XO

Praise for the series:

It was only a matter of time before a clever publisher realized that there is an audience for whom *Exile on Main Street* or *Electric Ladyland* are as significant and worthy of study as *The Catcher in the Rye* or *Middlemarch.* . . . The series . . . is freewheeling and eclectic, ranging from minute rock-geek analysis to idiosyncratic personal celebration—*The New York Times Book Review*

Ideal for the rock geek who thinks liner notes just aren't enough—*Rolling Stone*

One of the coolest publishing imprints on the planet—*Bookslut*

These are for the insane collectors out there who appreciate fantastic design, well-executed thinking, and things that make your house look cool. Each volume in this series takes a seminal album and breaks it down in startling minutiae. We love these. We are huge nerds—*Vice*

A brilliant series . . . each one a work of real love—*NME* (UK)

Passionate, obsessive, and smart—*Nylon*

Religious tracts for the rock 'n' roll faithful—*Boldtype*

[A] consistently excellent series—*Uncut* (UK)

We . . . aren't naive enough to think that we're your only source for reading about music (but if we had our way . . . watch out). For those of you who really like to know everything there is to know about an album, you'd do well to check out Continuum's "33 1/3" series of books—*Pitchfork*

For reviews of individual titles in the series, please visit our website at www.continuumbooks.com and 33third.blogspot.com

For more information on the 33 1/3 series,
visit 33third.blogspot.com.

For a complete list of books in the series,
see the back of this book.

XO

$33\frac{1}{3}$

Matthew LeMay

continuum

NEW YORK • LONDON

2009

The Continuum International Publishing Group Inc
80 Maiden Lane, New York, NY 10038

The Continuum International Publishing Group Ltd
The Tower Building, 11 York Road, London SE1 7NX

www.continuumbooks.com
33third.blogspot.com

Copyright © 2009 by Matthew LeMay

Library of Congress Cataloging-in-Publication Data
LeMay, Matthew.
XO / by Matthew LeMay.
p. cm. -- (33 1/3)
Includes bibliographical references.
ISBN-13: 978-0-8264-2900-1 (pbk. : alk. paper)
ISBN-10: 0-8264-2900-9 (pbk. : alk. paper)
1. Smith, Elliott, 1969-2003. XO. I. Title. II. Series.

ML420.S668L46 2009
782.42166092--dc22

2009006651

Table of Contents

Acknowledgments

Thank you Philip Fischer for your help, guidance, and insight. This book would not exist without you.

Thank you Larry Crane, Greg Di Gesu, Garrick Duckler, and Rob Schnapf for taking the time to speak with me.

And finally, thank you mom for your love and support.

Preface

Like many of his fans, I first encountered Elliott Smith when he performed "Miss Misery" at the Academy Awards ceremony on March 13, 1998. I was fourteen years old, and watching the Oscars with my parents had become a family ritual-by-default—not because of any particular interest in film, but rather because it was a rare chance for us all to share opinions on a subject where our spheres of cultural knowledge had some degree of overlap. I had never heard Elliott Smith's music before, but the sound of his name rang a vague, elusive note of recollection; I had *heard* of this guy before, but I couldn't place the name. As the camera focused in on a man standing uncomfortably in a white Prada suit, the significance of Smith's name suddenly returned to me. I turned to my parents and said, "Oh, this is Elliott Smith—now he's on the

Oscars and he's gonna be really famous, but he used to be this homeless junky who did HEROIN!" My father, whose cynicism was nectar to my junior-high mindset, let out a forced laugh and deadpanned, "you can tell."

I've listened to "Miss Misery" hundreds of times since then, and it's come to be one of my favorite Elliott Smith songs. As pop music goes, it is fairly undeniable; a strong melody, a great structural arc, unobtrusively clever and emotionally evocative lyrics. But the song I now know and love has no resemblance to the song I remember hearing during the Academy Awards. While it took a visit to YouTube for me to remember the visual component of Smith's performance, I have a distinct recollection of the song itself—or, rather, of a musical corollary to Smith's sad sack reputation. I couldn't even say where I had heard about Smith in the first place; likely a newspaper or a brief story on MTV or VH1. But my understanding of "Elliott Smith" not only colored my experience of his song—it effectively *created* a new song; a harsh, self-indulgent, and near-unlistenable ditty that lived in my memory and was almost impossible for me to shake.

It would be easy to write off my initial contact with Smith as a product of its particular time and context, or of my own immaturity. But even as I matured and

Smith's musical vocabulary expanded, I could not seem to get past my own illusory reading of "Miss Misery." As a musically ravenous high school student aware of Smith's reputation as a songwriter, I purchased *XO* in 1999, but never got into the record beyond a passing interest in its first single, "Waltz #2." I saw Smith at the Beacon Theater in 2001, and was taken aback by the professionalism and energy of his performance, but not enough so to spark any further interest in his recorded output. Later that year, I purchased Domino Records' box set of Smith's early work, primarily in an effort to win the affections of a girl whose AIM screen name was a combination of her given name and the letters "ESG" ("Elliott Smith Girl"). For a time, I listened obsessively to a CD by Smith's friends and collaborators Quasi—but I still felt an insurmountable distance between myself and any music that bore the name "Elliott Smith."

It was only when writing my band's second record in late 2005 that I truly began to bridge that distance. As a fledgling songwriter terrified of taking my lyrics too seriously, I had been writing exclusively from some semblance of "personal experience." But I was interested in the idea of using songs to literalize emotional observations; as a chance to say things via fictionalized characters that could never be said in person. In a conversation with a friend and bandmate, who grew up in Portland and was very familiar with Smith's music, *XO* came up as a record that does just that—an album that is unflinchingly harsh and emotionally direct, to the point of being difficult to listen to at times. For fear of looking stupid, I said "yeah"—we had discussed Smith's music in the past, and I wasn't ready to admit just how limited my interest actually was. But the conversation intrigued me—how could Elliott Smith, the poster boy for wallowing, mopey self-loathing, make a record that is unsparing, incisive, and . . . mean?

With that conversation in mind, I began reevaluating Smith's music, particularly *XO*. The ensuing process was gradual, but revelatory. Lines that had passed by suddenly stood out; characters that once seemed little more than one-dimensional projections of Smith himself were populated by fraught and contradictory emotions. The music itself grew richer and more complex, suddenly bursting with nuance, intelligence, and humor. Of *course* Smith's music fell short and failed to connect as weepy sad bastard music—it isn't.

When I sat down to write this book, I considered entirely omitting my dubious early impressions of Smith. But part of my fascination with Elliott Smith stems from this moment of misrecognition; from how Smith's cultural legacy seems perpetually at odds with the nature of his music. The "story" of Elliott Smith is that of a man with no agency; a mopey, weepy, druggy singer-songwriter plucked from coffeehouse obscurity to ambivalent semi-stardom by no effort of his own. *XO* is a work of incredible craft, intelligence, wit, and insight. In its lyrical concerns and its musical realization, it suggests that suffering does not create great art; that, instead, it leaves you "deaf and dumb and done." Far from a tear-stained journal entry, *XO* is a fully realized work of art.

As such, this is not a book that tells the *story* of Elliott Smith, or even a book that tells the *story* of Elliott Smith making *XO*. Countless stories of varying merit and tact have been written that begin "Steven Paul Smith was born in 1969 . . ." and I'm sure countless more will be written. In the particular case of *XO*, any effort to fix the record's meaning in Smith's biography seems thoroughly counter to the album's tone and mission. Telling the "real story" of Elliott Smith often serves only to emphasize his personal troubles, to place them above his craft and—given the sad and unsolved nature of his death—to cast a suspicious and dour pall over an incredible body of work.

Furthermore, telling the "real" story of a record almost invariably involves seeking out the "real" stories behind the songs, the "real" people the songs are about. Such information ostensibly exists regarding *XO*, but, as I will suggest in my analysis of the record, the songs on *XO* tended to veer *away* from personal details as Smith refined them. Understanding *XO* does not mean understanding Smith's personal pain—it means examining his tireless, impeccable craft.

In the first section of this book, I discuss how *XO* came to be, primarily by tracing the development of its songs. Though Smith was not given to discussing his work, he recorded more or less constantly, and many of the songs on *XO* are culminations of a fascinating sequence of demos and live performances, many of which have been widely circulated among fans. Obviously, any inferences made about the "creative process" are just that, but there are discernible trends in the development of *XO* that speak to the record's unique strengths. Specifically, I am interested in how *XO*'s lyrical content grew bolder, more incisive, and *less* tethered to personal experience as the album's production grew more professional and elaborate.

Smith's lyrical prowess, and his lyrical precision in particular, remain largely obfuscated by his reliance upon simple and unassuming language. And while Smith utilized a conventional and conversational pop song vocabulary, he mobilized common words to unique thematic ends. By drawing attention to his lyrics as meticulous, intentional writing—*not* simple confession—I attempt to shed light on some of the beliefs, ideas, and attitudes that permeate *XO*, especially those that explicitly contradict Smith's sup-posed biography.

In the second section of this book, I examine the cultural construct of "Elliott Smith"—how Smith was introduced to us via the media, and how the resultant construct was read against *XO*. Rather than simply dismissing the "Elliott Smith" produced by popular culture, I argue that it is important to analyze how this figure came to be, not only for understanding *XO*'s cultural legacy, but also for understanding how problematic concepts of "authenticity" and biography can color our understanding of music in general. The way we discuss artists matters—it changes and directs the way we hear and understand their work. In exam-ining the myth of "Elliott Smith," I attempt to pro-voke a wider discussion about agency, narrative, and craft.

Specifically, I seek to explore how Smith's position-ing as an "obscure singer-songwriter" and the story of his "sudden ascent" created contradictory demands and expectations that were often articulated and tenu-ously resolved via Smith's "personal life." Smith often spoke of the difference between personal turmoil and artistic craft, both on *XO* and in countless interviews conducted around the time of the album's release, but this troubling correlation often informed Smith's popular image, even in articles ostensibly refuting it.

I must admit that this book is meant to be something of a corrective; not to "set the record straight" about Elliott Smith's life, but rather to deemphasize his personal struggles and examine his craft. I can make no claim that any amount of research I could do would give me a window to the "real person" behind Smith's music. Furthermore, as Smith was well aware, knowing a "real person"—and that person's trials, tribulations, and failings—doesn't necessarily help you to understand that person's art. In fact, as my initial experience with Elliott Smith suggests, the illusion of such an understanding can lead to very limited and unsympathetic readings. In a 1999 interview with Spin Magazine, Smith said, "I don't like when people talk about all the bad things that have happened to them as if that makes them unique. Because I don't think I've had a harder time than other people." As a songwriter, Smith needs no excuses and no apologies. It is no coincidence that *XO* contains neither.

Part One—"Making Something From Nothing"

The "Story" of *XO*

Certain albums have fantastic back stories, rife with interpersonal turmoil, record industry intervention, and/or the birth or destruction of a local musical scene or cultural movement. *XO* is not one of those records. The extenuating circumstances directly leading up to the release of the album, which I will discuss briefly in the following pages, are almost maddeningly straightforward and unexciting. At the time of its release, *XO* constituted a substantial and logical step forward for Smith, aesthetically and occupationally, but it was by no means a sea change, nor was it in any way without precedent or contested by Smith, his label, or the majority of his fan base.

In the canon of Smith's work, *XO* is notable largely for being his "major label debut"—but that designation is in many ways misleading. In January of 1996, under the guidance of future manager Margaret Mittleman, Smith signed a music publishing deal with publishing giant BMG. Mittleman had made a name for herself in the music industry by signing then-largely-unknown Beck to a similar publishing deal in 1992, and would go on to be Smith's manager for a substantial portion of his career. Publishing deals such as those struck by Beck and Smith remain largely unexamined in the "major" vs. "indie" discussion, but have had a hand in some of the most creative albums made in the 1990s, including those by Built to Spill and Neutral Milk Hotel.

Rob Schnapf, who is both *XO*'s producer and Mittleman's husband, describes a publishing deal as follows:

> It was sort of like having a bank. You're selling part of your songs. A company is giving you money—it's sorta like you're getting equity out of your songs. So you sell 50% of your songs and you get a bunch of money. Whereas if you owned all of it, the money coming in would be all yours. But when you have a deal, you have to recoup whatever amount was advanced to you, and you share ownership. It's like a roll of the dice—the wisdom is, if you don't have to, you don't do it. But on the other hand it can really be

a great vehicle for helping you do a bunch of artist development type things. Especially if you're starting from ground zero.

While album royalties are generally thought of as the primary source of income for musicians, songwriting royalties can be much more lucrative, especially in the case of an artist like Smith whose work is played, performed, and covered extensively. Major labels are free to set up extremely unfavorable payment schemes regarding album royalties, but the basic terms of "mechanical" royalties and other songwriting fees are written into US copyright law, and as such are harder for labels to manipulate.

In a sense, then, a publishing deal such as Smith's necessitates that the artist relinquish a stake in one of his most reliable and potentially lucrative streams of income. But it also pays out in a creatively proactive way; while songwriting royalties can generate a steady flow of cash for an already-successful songwriter, Smith's publishing deal advanced him a sizeable sum of money in advance of each album's release ($25–30,000 per independent release and $50,000 per major label release). The timing of the deal, signed years before Smith's music would take on national prominence, was nothing short of perfect. With a steady salary from BMG, Smith was able to quit his day job and focus full-time on songwriting. Jackpot! Studio owner Larry Crane, who worked closely with Smith throughout the time that the deal was signed, recalls it having an immediate and noticeable effect on Smith's songwriting:

> I think that as soon as [the publishing deal was signed] he got better. I'm not much of an advocate of specu-lative music business practices, but it means he could stop doing drywall, doing that kind of work, and focus full-time on writing and recording. That gave us *Either/Or* and most of what later became *New Moon*.

Indeed, Smith's creative output seems to have sky-rocketed around the time that the publishing deal was signed. In Steve Hanft's 1998 documentary *Strange Parallel*, shot while Smith was living in New York City and working on *XO*, Smith succinctly summarized the benefits of being a professional songwriter: "it's better than laying gravel."

Smith's involvement with the world of "major labels" did not end with the BMG publishing deal; Smith's then-primary creative outlet Heatmiser released their final album *Mic City Sons* on Virgin offshoot Caroline Records in late 1996. The band's contract with Virgin included a "leaving member clause," giving the label first dibs on any of Smith's future solo output. As Smith pointed out in an interview with *Jim* magazine,

Heatmiser's contract with Virgin rendered it effectively impossible for Smith to continue releasing albums independently; either he would continue to release albums through Virgin, or he would be bought out of his contract by a label with sufficient capital—inevitably, a major.

Thus, while *XO* is the first Elliott Smith solo album to be released by a major label, it isn't exactly Smith's "major label debut." Still, Smith was a well-respected musician with a primarily local following signing to a large national label at a time when such labels were particularly suspect. The post-Nirvana "alternative" afterglow was fading, and many bands that had been signed in its wake were being unceremoniously dropped. If the record industry works in cycles of overenthusiastic speculation and frantic, destructive corrections, then 1997–1998 definitely qualifies as the latter.

In Smith's case, record industry turmoil may very well have worked to his advantage. In the wake of shake-ups, firings, drops, and mergers among major labels, a handful of smaller major-backed labels began to emerge in 1997, among them *V2* and David Geffen's DreamWorks. DreamWorks was founded by Geffen, Jeffrey Katzenberg, and Steven Spielberg, and was run by former Warner Brothers A&R giants Lenny Waronker and Mo Ostin, both of whom had been forced out of the label they helped to build. In both its

personnel and its rhetoric, DreamWorks seemed specifically geared toward responding to the rapid-fire
successions of signings and droppings by evoking the
language of "career artists" and "development."

Smith was both lucky and smart to sign to
DreamWorks at a time when the label had to put their
money where their proverbial mouth was. The label's
initial round of signings included artists like Smith,
Rufus Wainwright, and Henry Rollins, none of whom
were surefire hit makers. In an interview with the
Record Labels & Companies Guide Web site, former
DreamWorks A&R head Luke Wood described the
label's ethos:

> It takes time sometimes for people to reach their full
> potential. So what they try to do is highlight that
> potential, identify it, and stick with it. So I think
> in terms of the A&R process, if something is really
> great, if you can't stop thinking about it, then sign
> it. Work with it. Figure out a way to make it work
> in the marketplace. That is our number one prior-
> ity. It's not rhetoric. It's not lip service. It's really the
> way we do our job here. . . . With Mo, Michael, and
> Lenny, it's the exact same thing. At Warner Brothers,
> often they would stick with an artist like Neil Young,
> who would take two or three records to have a com-
> mercial hit. But the fact is, they always knew Neil
> would get to that place. I look at someone like Neil's
> career as a blueprint for someone who has ambitious

records—records that are somewhat creatively left of
the normal commercial voice—and at the same time
he has success. He has an enormous following.

Neil Young is perhaps the musician most commonly
invoked in the discourse of the "career artist;" a
musician with a large and aesthetically diverse catalog who doesn't necessarily produce a steady stream
of pop radio hits. Of course, this is the rhetoric that
all major labels tend to deploy, or at least all major
label A&R guys. Nobody wants to cop to being part
of a soulless marketing strategy, and the A&R guys
looking for "career artists" rarely last at their jobs for
long. (In 2003, the same year that DreamWorks was
declared a financial liability to its parent company and
sold off, there was talk of the label signing Backstreet
Boy-girlfriend Sarah Martin.)

Still, at the time of Smith's signing, he was in the
enviable position of being an artist genuinely admired
by a team of patient, experienced music business vet-
erans who, for the time being, had free rein over their
own company. The momentum behind Smith's signing segued seamlessly into the recording, release, and
promotion of *XO*. Between Smith's publishing deal
and his signing to DreamWorks, *XO* is a rare case of
the music business doing exactly what it is supposed to
do; discovering a remarkably talented artist, providing

financial backing so that artist can focus entirely on his craft, and ultimately bringing that artist's music to a wider audience. And while the more polished sound of *XO* did raise some eyebrows, all evidence suggests that the album's immaculate production was in no way a play by any industry force to make Smith more saleable. In an interview with *The Big Takeover*, Smith flatly rejected the insinuation that DreamWorks had any hand in *XO*'s creation:

> No, DreamWorks didn't know what I was going to do in the first place, and they didn't put any pressure on me at all. I could have made an acoustic record and they would have been fine with that. I think DreamWorks is trying to put out records they actually like. A lot of records get put out by labels just to make a lot of money. But DreamWorks have been really cool to me, so far.

Smith's "so far" betrays a bit of healthy skepticism; indeed, the suspicion of major label pressure on *XO* is understandable, but is not supported by anybody involved in the album's making. And, as Larry Crane suggests, any such pressure would have likely doomed the album:

> You couldn't produce him—he wouldn't have done those records if Rob and Tom had been really heavy-handed. . . . A lot of times people were like,

"you seem to kind of be at the spot where he was starting to add more to his songs—did you think it was weird?" And I'm like, "did you hear 'Pictures of Me'?" That and "Cupid's Trick" and "Christian Brothers"—they don't use that many elements, but they're really good arrangements. That was already happening. If you gave him 16 tracks or you gave him 24 tracks, he'd start adding more stuff. . . . He had a gift for really good arrangement and adding stuff on to the song.

There are some really clueless fuckers out there who hear *XO* and think that Rob and Tom added stuff, or that the label did. I know where those overdubs came from—and I think there are even little bits, like, "Elliott complained about the Beatles piano on 'Baby Britain,' and the producers added that." And it's like—of course not, he recorded it at Jackpot! With Joanna! That's *his* part! Nobody was hovering over him telling him how to make this one way or another. Rob and Tom were both very sympathetic producers to work with, and very competent engineers as well. They never would have pushed it in any direction other than what Elliott wanted.

Indeed, the "direction" of *XO* seems to have been determined long before Smith signed to DreamWorks. Schnapf suggests that *Either/Or could* have been a more produced record in the style of *XO*; the decision to hold back had less to do with monetary or time constraints, and more to do with Smith wishing to follow through the record as it was originally conceived and recorded:

> When we were working on *Either/Or*, there were times when we started to build things up more instrumentally, or talked about doing more elaborate stuff. It could have very easily gone there but this seemed to be a transitional record for Elliott. He saw what it could be but wasn't yet comfortable with that. So it was sort of a step into the pool as opposed to jumping all the way in.

Schnapf and Tom Rothrock, who would go on to produce *XO* (and who had co-produced Heatmiser's swan song *Mic City Sons*) also produced a good deal of *Either/Or*, mixing, overdubbing, and at times rebuilding Smith's songs from scratch. Though it does not immediately resemble the more "hi-fi" *XO*, *Either/Or* is similarly rich and varied in texture and instrumentation, a remarkable balancing act between rough-edged material and precise, spacious mixing. I've heard some truly stellar live versions of *Either/Or* opener "Speed Trials," but the album version (a 4-track recording of Smith's mixed with Schnapf and Rothrock), with its tape hiss and ringing snare drum, still sounds absolutely perfect.

Smith himself was always a remarkably capable and intuitive engineer, regardless of the limited and inconsistent equipment at his disposal. Smith had amassed a modest collection of microphones and outboard equipment at the house he shared with his bandmates in Heatmiser from the summer of 1995 to the summer of 1996, but interpersonal and creative tensions rendered it a less-than-ideal place to get work done. An extra room at JJ Gonson's Undercover, Inc space and Smith's own basement both served as functional places to record, but when Larry Crane opened Jackpot! Recording Studio in February of 1997, it provided Smith with a home base—a comfortable and familiar studio in which Smith could record at his own pace and hone his skill as an engineer. Crane, who had interviewed Smith for his *Tape Op* 'zine in 1996 and tracked vocals for "Pictures of Me" that same year at his home studio, recalls hearing of Smith's wish to open a space similar to Jackpot!:

> Before I started Jackpot!, [Elliott] was talking about "I've gotta move into a space and get a 16-track and just be able to work," so Rebecca Gates [of the Spinanes] put us together and said, "you guys need to talk, because you're doing the same thing." I was like, "Oh hey, there's no reason for us to both build studios and one of them to be empty half the time." So he helped me find the space and move in our gear. I loved Elliott as a person—when we started off, he was just helping me build this studio and was gonna work out of there and stuff. And we became friends

out of that, and to just check everything we started recording his stuff. "Let's test the 8-track see if that works."

And those early things, from the first year of operation at Jackpot! were things like "Amity," "Baby Britain," "Cecilia/Amanda" and "Miss Misery." I remember we did demos for a handful of songs, instrumental demos that didn't have any vocal, where he hadn't written the lyrics yet. Just sketching stuff out to see if the parts sat together. But I gotta admit, there was never much discussion about whether something was a demo, or if it was for a record. It was just, "hey, do you want to record something?" And I would just try to do the best job that I could. He would sneak in there and do stuff at night—"All Cleaned Out," "I Didn't Understand," stuff that I didn't even know.

Smith's busy touring schedule in 1997 did substantially eat into the time he could use to record at Jackpot!. But, according to Crane, that did not stop Smith from continuing to meticulously demo the songs that would become *XO*:

So he was on tour for weeks, months—and then he came back, threw some stuff in the back of the studio, and then went back on the road. There was little downtime—and I don't know when and how he would've recorded some of these things. That's what I mean about these [*XO*] demos. I'm sure he'd be somewhere else, if somebody had home recording equipment or the most rudimentary anything, he'd be like "here's my chance!"

By the time Smith was signed to DreamWorks in early 1998, he had recorded dozens of demos for the songs that would become *XO*, and had road-tested many of them as well. When Smith did not have time to demo a song in its entirety, or when the lyrics were not finished when the initial demo was recorded, he would often record two different demos of a song: one bare-bones acoustic and/or electric guitar and vocal demo, and one instrumental demo with full instrumentation. The purpose of the former was to sketch the broad outlines of the song, establishing its melody and chordal structure. The purpose of the latter was to make sure that the instrumental arrangement of each song held its own and worked properly.

Before entering Sunset Sound in early 1998 to commence work on *XO*, Smith compiled a Digital Audio Tape (DAT) of demo versions, labeled with the album's earlier title: *Grand Mal*. (According to the *Big Takeover* interview, the album was originally to be called *XO*, but Smith deemed the title too close to *Either/Or* and renamed it *Grand Mal*, only to be contacted by a band with that same name and change it back.) The tracklist for this DAT is as follows:

"Waltz #1" Demo
"Better Off Than Dead" ["Sweet Adeline"] Instrumental
"Cecilia/Amanda" Demo
"Anything Is Better Than Nothing" ["New Monkey"]
    Organ Intro
"Anything Is Better Than Nothing" ["New Monkey"]
    Instrumental
"I Didn't Understand" Acoustic Guitar Demo
"Waltz #2" Demo [Full Band]
"Baby Britain" Instrumental
"Amity" Rough Mix
"Memory Lane" Rough Demo
"Bottle Up and Explode" Demo
"Bled White" Acoustic Guitar Demo
"Baby Britain" Acoustic Guitar Demo
"Better Off Than Dead" ["Sweet Adeline"] Acoustic
    Guitar Demo

Crane suggests that this DAT was likely assembled to give those involved in the making of *XO* a sense of where the songs were going. An early tracklisting for *Grand Mal*, dating from prior to the Sunset sessions, offers further insight into Smith's original conception of the record, in which the two "Waltzes" each kick off a "side" of the record:

"Waltz #1"
"Better Off than Dead" ["Sweet Adeline"]

"Cecilia/Amanda"
"Anything Is Better Than Nothing" ["New Monkey"]
"I Didn't Understand"
"Waltz #2"
"Baby Britain"
"Amity"
"Memory Lane"
"Bottle Up and Explode"
"Bled White"

Thus, when Smith finally entered the studio to record *XO*, he was armed not only with an extensive backlog of demo recordings, but with a clear idea of the record he intended to craft as well. Obviously, this initial tracklist changed substantially over the course of recording *XO*. As it happens, these changes were not often discussed, but rather executed intuitively by Smith over the course of the album's recording. Crane, who has gone on to record countless bands at Jackpot!, describes how such in-studio discussions are less common than some may think:

> I think one perception is that there are a lot of discussions in the studio—but I think that one thing that's always forgotten is that certain outside factors always dictate what's going on—and one of those is budget. So you might say, "okay, we've got a couple weeks in the studio," and you have 15 songs or whatever—you just have to get down to work. You can't sit down and

go "how's this record gonna feel?" In general, you just kinda get to work. You've got a budget, you've got time, maybe the players are only there for a certain time. And Elliott was always good at just getting to work.

Schnapf echoes this sentiment, suggesting that many of the production choices that went into *XO* were "natural" to Smith, and were not discussed at length. Indeed, Smith's approach to writing and recording is not written in conversations—it is written in the work itself. Part of what makes Smith's body of work so immersive—and part of what made researching this book feel like an archaeological dig—is that the clues to his creative process lie buried in an impressive pile of demos, outtakes, and live recordings.

Smith's reworking of *XO* continued right up until its release. On June 15, 1998, when the majority of recording for *XO* had already taken place, the album was prepared for mastering with the following tracklist:

"Tomorrow, Tomorrow"
"Waltz #2"
"Baby Britain"
"Pitseleh"
"Everybody Cares, Everybody Understands"

"Bled White"
"Waltz #1"
"Amity"
"Oh Well, Okay"
"Bottle Up and Explode"
"A Question Mark"
"Sweet Adeline"
"I Didn't Understand"

Noticeably absent from this sequence is "Independence Day," the result of a later session intended to produce b-sides for the record. (This session also produced *Figure 8* highlight "Happiness," as well as the instrumental b-side "Our Thing.")

Imagining *XO* with this tracklist speaks to how effective its final sequencing is; while "I Didn't Understand" retains its logical place at the record's end, "Sweet Adeline" makes little sense as the album's penultimate track, and the epic coda of "Everybody Cares, Everybody Understands" stands to be a momentum-killer so close to the album's start. According to Crane, Smith struggled with *XO*'s sequencing, and ultimately enlisted the help of his close friend and one-time girlfriend Joanna Bolme to finalize the album's running order.

The culmination of a year-long process of writing, recording, and reworking, *XO* was released by DreamWorks Records on August 25, 1998.

XO Song by Song

Though Elliott Smith was never particularly interested in discussing his own music, he did often speak about the music he enjoyed. When interviewed about Elvis Costello for a VH1 special, Smith described him as someone who "really likes words." In a 1998 interview with *Interview* magazine, Smith described his own songwriting process in similar terms:

> [I like] music, just the sound of things. That's my favorite thing. I love words and it's good to love words if you are going to sing them, but the bottom line is the way something sounds. Sometimes I'll compromise a lyric before I'll compromise the way something sounds, even though I hate doing that.

Of course, every songwriter has a different idea of what "sounds good." Some favor lyrics that operate smoothly and seamlessly within tightly structured songs, others favor lyrics that expand, destabilize, and rupture their musical context. Smith definitely falls into the former category, thriving within the formal constraints of pop music. The majority of actual language Smith utilizes is the bread and butter of pop songwriting: "head," "love," "picture," ambiguous "you"s and "she"s, etc. Many of Smith's lyrics are so seamless—so formally and linguistically unobtrusive—that they easily go by unnoticed, failing to register *as* lyrics, let alone the kind that warrant any sort of analysis.

Thus, upon a cursory listen, Smith's craft and discipline threaten to read as a simple lack of sophistication. The opposite is, in fact, true—the more outwardly unassuming Smith's lyrics are, the more likely it is that those lyrics are the result of countless revisions and reworkings. When asked by *The Big Takeover* whether he works on making his lyrics more "song-like," Smith responded: "More 'song-like' to me equals more speaking-like. I like, if possible, to write the way that people actually speak. That's why when people bring up comparisons to poetic singer/songwriters it gets on my nerves. I don't feel as flowery!"

Smith's skepticism toward the "poetic singer/ songwriter" figure goes beyond a simple distaste for "flowery" language. In a frequently Myspace'd May 1998 interview with a Dutch TV station, Smith described his wariness toward "manipulative" lyrics:

> The thing that's kind of a drag about the singer-songwriter tag is that it has this connotation of being super-sentimental, kinda manipulative lyrically, as if the person singing is trying to get everybody to feel just like them. But there's a big difference between describing . . . I mean, you take a picture of New York and one person will look at it and think that it's really

depressing and frightening, and another person will look at it and think of all the fun things you could do . . . I think songs are kind of like that.

Smith's wish to avoid the "manipulative" tropes of singer-songwriterdom is evident throughout *XO*. Smith does not, as many singer-songwriters do, structure his songs around his own (real or fictional) life. Many songwriters evoke broad philosophical and psychological themes to explain or justify the their personal emotions; Smith (or, rather Smith-as-narrator) offers personal emotions as a jumping off point for addressing broad philosophical and psychological themes. The tone of Smith's lyrics is generally observational, and tends to involve a multiplicity of subjectivities and perspectives.

Smith's interest in leaving his songs open to multiple interpretations is well documented, and best expressed in his oft-stated answer to the oft-asked question of whether or not he is a "folk" singer. When asked this question during an extremely awkward interview with MTV's Carson Daly, Smith responded: "Folk is just a style. Folk usually has one point, and it's usually a moral. Whereas pop, a song can mean nothing or it can mean lots of things, and no one can be sure which ones they are." Smith echoed that sentiment in an interview with Yahoo.com: "Folk singers usually have a clear point to their songs . . . And they usually involve a moralistic point about something you ought to do, or ought not to do, or about some injustice that's been done to somebody. I don't write like that."

In closely analyzing *XO* and its lyrics, my goal is not to somehow "fix" the meaning of Smith's songs. Instead, I offer a reading of *XO* in the hopes of *un*fixing some of the meanings that have been consistently and problematically tethered to Smith's imagined biography. In tracing the development of the songs that became *XO*, I hope to draw attention to the remarkable process by which Smith created, honed and refined his work. In examining Smith's lyrics, I hope to emphasize the themes and concerns that specifically run *counter* to problematic biographical interpretations of *XO*.

In an excellent 1998 interview with *Magnet*, Smith explained how his use of drug addiction terminology—the theme in Smith's music perhaps most commonly assumed to be rooted in his "life story"—is *not*, in fact, a matter of simple biographical transposition:

> The thing that's fun for me is to make parallels between things. That's more interesting to me, at the moment anyway, than writing really straight songs about a particular person or event. Metaphors work a lot better when you don't draw attention to the fact that they're metaphors. Talking about drugs—and

why people do drugs and how they feel about it—just leads you to the same things as talking about relationships and people in love . . . [When I wrote "The White Lady Loves You More"], Drugs were on my mind, but they weren't only on my mind because of my involvement with them. . . . They were partly on my mind because it's a very useful device to talk about other things that are harder to name. If you can't name the big thing, you have to break it apart into small things with names and build it back up using the small things.

Indeed, to whatever extent Smith's experience with drugs may have sparked his interest in the subject matter, he uses the language of drug addiction as a means of outward reflection, not inward confession. And yet, as he told *Magnet*, he never made a point of announcing these rhetorical maneuvers within the songs themselves. In the second issue of his fantastic *Last Plane to Jakarta* 'zine, John Darnielle wrote of *XO* as an album that does not draw attention to its own lyrical complexities:

While *XO* doesn't require the magnifying glass called for by *Roman Candle*, it's hardly written in the universal language, either, and while those willing to meet a song halfway will find it heavy with poignant moments and a few truly breathtaking sequences, it's easy to imagine Elliott Smith getting pink-slipped at the end of his contract. It's a pity, because he should be loved and praised for his vision, and he should be well paid for his great originality. It usually doesn't work that way, though, so in all probability Elliott Smith's career will wind up as one more object-lesson in how unfair the world is. None of which makes any difference in the final analysis. *XO* is a great record, plain and simple. It doesn't need your love, but it deserves it.

Perhaps the most remarkable thing about *XO* is that it doesn't *ask* for your love; Smith's performances, as with his lyrics, wholly lack the cues that singer-songwriters (a term I use here as an occupational, not aesthetic, description) will often drop to draw attention to their craft, particularly the "this is a clever lyric" panache that makes a small handful of "clever" pop singers so compelling, and many more of them so insufferable. Excepting the works of those songwriters who have owned and mastered this irony (Morrissey, Stephin Merritt, etc.), any gesture at a song's own greatness vastly and irreparably diminishes it.

I am hard pressed to think of a single singer-songwriter as lyrically *or* musically clever as Smith who showed so little interest in projecting the brilliance and sophistication of his music back onto himself. For Smith, singing always seemed like a disembodied act, an earnest attempt to generate something that could exist apart from its creator and, in turn, speak for itself. In the coming pages, I attempt to trace the process by which Smith gave voice to the fourteen astonishing songs that constitute *XO*.

"Sweet Adeline"

Though *XO* is more ornate than Smith's earlier solo records, the album's first aesthetic departure is a subtractive one: the lack of a double-tracked lead vocal. In his earlier recordings, Smith would often work by recording one take of guitar and vocals, then almost-duplicating that take, in effect doubling both the guitar and vocal lines. When Smith's voice enters fifteen seconds into "Sweet Adeline," it stands alone, naked, singular and upfront. Technically speaking, Smith was by no means a tremendously gifted singer; he had a fairly limited range and was not given to any sort of theatrics. But on "Sweet Adeline," his voice sounds strong and certain. He is pitch-perfect, sings clearly, and ends each line with an elegant vibrato, a performance that effortlessly rises to the meet the song's pristine production.

Lyrically, Smith opens *XO* with an invocation: "Cut this picture into you and me / burn it backwards, kill this history." This presence of the word "cut" suggests a separation; "cut up this picture of us so as to separate you from me." But the line also invites a reading that is more ontological than relational; Smith is not only singing about the relationship between "you" and "me," but also about the difference between "you and me" and a pictorial representation. "Pictures" appear frequently in Smith's oeuvre, often as a way of expressing sensory distance and isolation. Indeed, throughout *XO*, the language of the romantic pop song (as well as language typically used to describe drug addiction) is used primarily as a jumping off point for broader conceptual explorations. Smith never really says who "you" and "me" are—situational and personal specificity is beside the point.

These opening lines of "Sweet Adeline" introduce a wary and fearful view of the past that permeates *XO*. Smith continues the song's opening verse: "make it over, make it stay away / Or hate will sing the ending that love started to say." Here, the past is set up as a threat to the future; whatever love has started to say, the presence of this "picture" or "history" threatens to not only disrupt it, but to turn love into its dreaded antithesis. Additionally, the act of speaking is ascribed to love, the act of singing ascribed to hate. In keeping with Smith's skepticism toward the "singer-songwriter" role and "flowery" language, direct communication is privileged and artifice is suspect.

As with many of Smith's songs (including "Miss Misery"), "Sweet Adeline" segues from an emotionally specific but narratively broad opening verse to a dream-like second verse:

> There's a kid a floor below me saying
> "Brother can you spare sunshine for a brother,
>   old man winter's in the air"
> Walked me up a story, asking how you are
> Told me not to worry, you were just a shooting star

This segment is typical of Smith's more surreal passages, introducing a character who is given no narrative pretext yet seems to possess some kind of knowledge or relevance. Matching tone to content, Smith sings "asking how you are" as a more casual "asking how ya are," marking his tendency to deliver bits of conversation in a more casual voice. Indeed, for a singer often described by both fans and detractors as essentially expressionless, Smith shows a remarkable sensitivity to the relationship between lyrics and performance.

Throughout the second verse of "Sweet Adeline," a lone organ part oscillates above Smith's guitar and vocals, musically mirroring the verse's "shooting star." As the verse concludes, this organ line quietly subsides, leaving room for a momentary bass swell to usher in an explosion of drums, piano, and guitar. The fanciful piano chords immediately following the song's walloping chorus (which slyly nods to Smith's song

"Clementine,") evoke the British Music Hall tradition
mined by the Beatles and Elvis Costello, among countless others, announcing definitively that this is *not*
going to be a "singer-songwriter" record, in aesthetic
or in musical approach. The rollicking, propulsive chorus settles into a fleshed out third verse:

> It's a picture-perfect evening and I'm staring
>   down the sun
> Fully loaded, deaf and dumb and done
> Waiting for sedation to disconnect my head
> Or any situation where I'm better off than dead

This verse, often harped on for its "better off than dead"
lyric (which was, thankfully, not ultimately used as the
song's title), reintroduces the "picture" as figure of dis-
sociation from the present; there is more than a little bit
of irony to Smith's use of the phrase "picture-perfect."
The evening's idyllic description frames Smith's feeling of disconnection; the sensory deprivation of being
"deaf and dumb and done." (A phrase Smith revisits in
XO's second track, "Tomorrow, Tomorrow.")

It is worth noting that "Sweet Adeline" is far from a
structurally conventional song, sporting three verses
and a single chorus that echoes the song's introduc-
tion in melody and feel. It is also deceptively complex
rhythmically, from the momentum-building piano
figures in its chorus to the stray hi-hat sixteenth notes

in its third verse. Though no early demos of "Sweet Adeline" have leaked to the public, the song's airtight arrangement was a long time in the making; Crane recalls seeing similarly arranged versions of its music dating back as far as 1989.

"Tomorrow, Tomorrow"

"Tomorrow, Tomorrow" is one of a handful of songs that developed almost entirely during the *XO* sessions at Sunset Sound. Schnapf recalls seeing the song come to life after setting Elliott up with a uniquely tuned "high-strung" guitar:

> For "Tomorrow, Tomorrow" he had that guitar bit [during the song's introduction]. I'm sure it was kicking around—I don't think anything just flew out of him. But the vision definitely came in the studio, when it was like, "oh! It'll go like this, then this, let's roll"—and then boom! He was playing it one way and then I had my 12-string strung like a high-strung, where you get a set of 12 strings and you take off all the low strings, so it winds up being a really close-voiced, more piano-y kinda thing. Except for I leave the unisons on, the E and the B.

By leaving the unison strings on, Schnapf effectively provided Smith with a pre-doubled acoustic guitar. Like "Sweet Adeline," "Tomorrow, Tomorrow" begins with the sound of that guitar unaccompanied. But while the acoustic guitar figure on "Sweet Adeline" is shapely and directional, "Tomorrow, Tomorrow" is more textural and tense.

Lyrically, "Tomorrow, Tomorrow" starts on similarly impressionistic terrain:

> Everybody knows which way you go
> Straight to over
> No one wants to see you inside of me
> Straight to over

"Straight to over" is a fairly unwieldy line to repeat; the vowel sound in "to" is essentially lost to the long "o" in "over" (a contraction that effectively mirrors the line itself). Smith continues:

> I heard the hammer at the lock
> Say you're deaf and dumb and done
> Give yourself another talk
> This time make it sound like someone

Again, Smith uses the phrase "deaf and dumb and done" to describe a character who is stuck in an internal world; the "hammer at the lock" literalizing an external force trying to break through that sealed off façade. The second two lines of the verse are telling as well, presumably instructing someone to make his/her self-directed pep talks more believable—or at least more believably grounded in a perspective other than his/her own. Characteristically, this passage is vague on details but specific in emotional resonance; Smith delivers "make it sound like someone," a line that introduces an extraneous syllable to the song's rhythmic structure, with just the right degree of conversational contempt to enhance its affective valence without disrupting the song's flow.

"Tomorrow, Tomorrow" sets up a framework for past, present, and future that carries through the entire record. "Tomorrow" is a place of uncertainty on *XO*, and it is often where the bad influences of the past and the bad decisions of the present come to fruition and inflict harm. The song's second verse speaks to this danger:

> The noise is coming out
> And if it's not out now
> Then tomorrow, tomorrow
> They took your life apart
> And called your failures art
> They were wrong, though
> They won't know 'till tomorrow

"They took your life apart and called your failures art / They were wrong, though" is perhaps the most illuminating line on the record, its most direct and clearly stated assertion that great suffering does not create great art. Smith's caveat that "they won't know 'til tomorrow," again sets up the future as a place of potential consequence—the worst results of your failures are yet to come.

As the song's lyrics become more concrete, the musical arrangement is subtly but effectively fleshed out. When, in the third verse, Smith intones, "I've got static in my head / The collected sounds of everything," the word "everything" is delivered in a soaring three-part harmony that recalls Crosby, Stills, and Nash—the kind of understated musical payoff that can drastically elevate a song that is fairly consistent in structure and dynamics. Smith continues:

> Tried to go to where it led
> But it didn't lead to anything
> The noise is coming out
> And if it's not out now
> I know it's just about
> To drown tomorrow out

The "static in [Smith's] head" ("head" being used, as it is throughout *XO*, very specifically to represent the rational mind) speaks to the confusion of the present; Smith tries to follow "the collected sound of everything" to a distinct future, but it doesn't lead anywhere—it is incoherent and irreconcilable. One can read the last word(s) of the song's penultimate line as "about" or "a bout." Following the first reading, the future is perpetually self-nullifying. Following the second reading, the present is perpetually sacrificed to stave off the future. Either way, "tomorrow" is left obscured and uncertain.

"Waltz #2" (*XO*)

It has been suggested that Smith wrote "Waltz #2" about a memory of his mother and her husband singing Karaoke at a Texas bar. According to Crane, Smith's relationship with his mother was not fodder for musical confession, but rather a personal starting point for broader issues to be broached:

> I think he used archetypes. And he definitely played with his relationship with his mom, and build on that, using that character as a basis for an idea. I think he could look at things with a kind of cold eye sometimes. He read a lot of philosophy. When people are searching with him for a sort of confessional songwriting thing, you're getting maybe a little piece of that, but you're also getting this deeper look at who people really are. It was real writing.

Indeed, tracing the song's development through early live performances, it is clear that "Waltz #2" grew away from personal references as it grew more

emotionally coherent. During one of the song's earliest performances on July 17, 1997, Smith's lyrics were
notably different, and seem more rooted in childhood
memory:

> Holds the mic like a big cigarette, singing
> "Cathy's Clown"
> While the man she's married to now knocks
> another untouchable down
> You appear composed, so you are I suppose—who
> can really tell?
> 'Cause you show no emotion at all, stare into space
> like a dead china doll
>
> I'm never gonna know you now, but I'm gonna
> love you anyhow
>
> Now she's done and they're calling someone—
> I recognize the name
> But my memory of him is remote, and I'm doing
> just fine, hour to hour, note to note
> He's gonna have his revenge pretty soon—
> "You're No Good"
> "You're no good, you're no good, you're no good"—
> can't you tell that it's well understood?
>
> I'm never gonna know you now, but I'm gonna
> love you anyhow
> Here today, expected to stay on and on and on—
> I'm tired, so tired
>
> Looking out on a substitute scene where we belong
> Me and my mom, trying to pretend that you're wrong

In subsequent live versions, "me and my mom" becomes "I love you, mom" and "trying to pretend that you're wrong" reverts to "it's ok, it's alright, nothing's wrong." (A manuscript from mid-1997, reprinted in Autumn de Wilde's *Elliott Smith*, suggests that this line was originally written as it finally appeared on *XO*.) The later inclusion of the greeting "XO, mom" inscribes an act of writerly distance, taking Smith's statement of denial—and, in turn, his perspective within the song—out of his memory and into the present. There is a noticeable shift in subjectivity over the course of "Waltz #2"'s development, as the direct address of Smith's initial lyrics gives way to third-person pronouns. In enacting such a change, Smith further carves out a place of isolated observation, rendering the song's chorus all the more poignant.

From this place of detachment, Smith is able to articulate many of *XO*'s recurring themes. In the song's second verse, he once again speaks to the dangers of the past:

> Now she's done and they're calling someone—
>   such a familiar name
> I'm so glad that my memory's remote
> 'cause I'm doing just fine, hour to hour, note to note

The change from "I recognize the name" to "such a familiar name" playfully invokes the familial element of Smith's memory (familiar / familial), but also enriches the word "calling" (calling someone for their turn to sing a song vs. calling someone a name via that song). Smith's assertion that he's "doing just fine, hour to hour, note to note" does not suggest the same self-delusion as "it's okay, it's alright, nothing's wrong," owing in part to the lyrics that precede it, and in part to the subtle expressive cues of Smith's performance. It is well in keeping with the lyrical constructs of *XO* that the distance of memory would allow for things to be—however tenuously and temporarily—"just fine."

As Smith honed the lyrics to "Waltz #2," his delivery developed as well; the transition from "I recognize the name" to "such a familiar name" omits the awkward pickup of the "I," emphasizing the upward dynamic of the line even in acoustic performances. In the earliest live versions of "Waltz #2," "stares into space like a dead china doll" is sung with a choppy, metered cadence; "stares into space [pause] like a dead [pause] china doll." By an August 1998 performance in Oregon, the first half of the line is delivered more smoothly, and by a May 1998 performance at Portland's La Luna, while the recording of *XO* was well underway, the line is delivered more closely to how it is sung on the record. Though the seamless phrasing of *XO* seems natural and easy, it is the end result of a long process of revision, trial, and error.

Musically, the basics of "Waltz #2" do not seem to have changed much over the song's numerous lyrical revisions. In an interview with *Guitar Player*, Smith described his affinity for the type of chord change that gives life to "Waltz #2":

> I'm kind of a sucker for passing chords, such as when you play a progression like G, D with an F# in the bass, and F. There's a half-step, descending melody in those types of sequences that I love. The Beatles did that a lot. And that's what I really like about traditional music. There are ways in which the chords connect to each other—where certain notes only move a little bit while the main notes move a lot. Anything that has an ascending or descending half-step thing in it always ropes me in.

The progression in "Waltz #2"'s chorus from an F to a C with an E in the bass highlights just such a half-step descending melody, adding a sense of fragile tension to Smith's vocal line. Smith's piano part, echoing his vocal melody and anticipating the song's rhythmic ebbs and flows, further develops its sense of momentum. "Waltz #2"'s arrangement clearly evokes a live band, but as the song's only performer, Smith was free to arrange as he saw fit without bruising anybody's ego; instruments could come and go to suit the song, without concern for what the drummer would do during the quiet parts.

"Baby Britain"

"Baby Britain" is one of two songs on *XO* that was recorded primarily at Jackpot! during the sessions that produced numerous *XO* demos and b-sides. Initially, engineering credit was given to Crane, but "Baby Britain" was in fact tracked by Smith's then-girlfriend Joanna Bolme. (Bolme, who was learning recording techniques from Smith and Crane at the time, would go on to engineer a number of albums at Jackpot! herself.) Indeed, the instrumental tracks themselves are not quite as hi-fi as the majority of *XO*, but in Schnapf's words, "the vibe was there."

"Baby Britain" is an unsparing character sketch dressed up as an immaculate, Beatlesque pop song. Over bouncy piano chords and guitar stabs, Smith introduces us to the song's titular character:

> Baby Britain feels the best floating over a sea of vodka
> Separated from the rest, fights problems with
>   bigger problems
> Sees the ocean fall and rise, counts the waves that
>   somehow didn't hit her
> Water pouring from her eyes, alcoholic and
>   very bitter

The imagery expands and contracts; vodka forms a sea, problems are fought with bigger problems, the ocean falls and rises, tears pour from Baby Britain's eyes. A similar dynamic is utilized in the song's second verse, which evokes the miniature ("dead soldiers lined up on the table") and the monumental ("London bridge"). It is worth noting that Smith sings the line "fall and rise" to a melody that first descends and then ascends. In both his lyrics and his melodies, Smith displays a keen awareness of movement and scale; even as it throbs and undulates, "Baby Britain" is unerringly exact.

The song's chorus offers perhaps the best possible example of Smith's formal discipline contrasting his lyrical incisiveness—"for someone half as smart / you'd be a work of art" is an extremely simple and palatable couplet, to the point where it can easily pass by unnoticed. But it is a scathing sentiment, and one that echoes the themes of responsibility (and lack thereof) that permeate the song and the record at large. Similarly, the closing line of the chorus—"I can't help you until you start"—alludes to the futility of trying to help somebody who is not amenable to such intervention—a theme that Smith revisits extensively later in *XO*.

As with many of Smith's songs (including "Between the Bars" and "Cecilia/Amanda"), "Baby Britain" tells of a character who fails to live up to her potential. In an interview with *The Big Takeover*, Smith articulated a view on these matters that is at both sympathetic and pragmatic:

> I think no one ever lives up to their potential, and that's not a negative thing, though it sounds like that in my songs. I mean, it does burn me out sometimes. But it's impossible to live up to your potential in this world because if you can, potential itself is not worth very much. People are infinitely more capable than what they end up showing.

In other words, potential is valuable *only* because it always exceeds that which is actually accomplished—if we all lived up to our potential, the very concept of "potential" would cease to exist. This view likely accounts in part for Smith's creative restlessness and commendable work ethic; however close he came to fully realizing his artistic goals, there was always room to grow and work to be done.

"Baby Britain" was released as the second single from *XO*, in a slightly remixed version that retains its backbeat through every chorus. (Judging from the version I have, the single is also mastered slightly louder than *XO*, a necessary concession to radio airplay that thankfully was not applied to the album itself.) The decision to release an edited version of "Baby Britain" could be seen as a disruptive artistic intervention on behalf of DreamWorks, but if anything, it seems inconsequentially misguided. At worst, the changes made to "Baby Britain" simply compromise one of the many structural elegances of a song that is still irresistible whether writ large or examined in detail.

"Pitseleh"

In both its tone and its placement on *XO*, "Pitseleh" always strikes me as an interesting counterpoint to "Between the Bars," a song occupying a similar spot on *Either/Or*. In terms of sheer ubiquity, "Between the Bars" seems to have surpassed "Miss Misery" as Elliott Smith's most popular song. And it is definitely among his best. But, as with "Baby Britain," its formal perfection masks its emotional complexity. In the song's central lyrical conceit, Smith is the one on the *outside* of the bars, looking in. Many have interpreted the line "drink up, baby" to mean that the song is "about" substance abuse, but as is often the case in Smith's writing, the drink itself is just a means to an end. "Between the Bars" is a song about using emotional intelligence as a mechanism of control; of maintaining and perpetuating a dysfunctional relationship for the power it gives you.

In its chorus, "Between the Bars" imitates a love song, but reveals a startling darkness underneath:

> The people you've been before that you don't want
>   around anymore
> They push and shove and won't bend to your will
> I'll keep them still

One can choose to read a comma before the word "still," but either way, this chorus is not a lover's sweet and generous offer of understanding, nor does it somehow defer responsibility onto the specter of alcoholism. It is intimate, but horribly so—a gesture of control in which a person's past selves are maintained and manipulated by their partner. Whether Smith is promising to "keep them still" or "keep them, still," he is still promising to keep them around.

In a sense, "Pitseleh" can be read as the aftermath of "Between the Bars," a cautionary tale written in hindsight that implicitly warns of the dangers that can come of accepting emotional responsibility for another. Lyrically, it is one of the most strikingly direct and sad songs Smith has written. The song's evocative opening couplet: "I'll tell you why I don't want to know where you are / I've got a joke I've been dying to tell you" is mirrored and elucidated by a line later in the song: "I was bad news for you just because / I never meant to hurt you." The two halves of this line can either be read independently or as part of one clause. One way the song speaks to the dangers of good intentions, the other it speaks to the arbitrary nature of bad outcomes.

Noticeably absent from "Pitseleh" is the word "sorry," which seems to be the shortest way to encapsulate the tension between "I never meant to hurt you" and "I was bad news for you." The closest Smith comes to an outright apology is the decidedly impersonal "no one deserves it." It is rather shocking for a song utilizing the aesthetic most commonly associated with the "singer-songwriter" to reject the notion of interpersonal causality, the ideological core of any "I did you wrong" or "you did me wrong" song. Indeed, throughout *XO*, Smith grapples with the question of whether or not anyone can really help or hurt anyone else. In the song's second verse, Smith masterfully relinquishes his own position in this equation: "I'm not what's missing from your life now / I could never be the puzzle pieces." This is not a matter of simple self-deprecation—it is a rejection of the romantic illusion that one person can rescue another, an illusion that sees its dark and destructive outcome in "Between the Bars."

Smith's assertion that "no one deserves it" ushers in one of the most jaw-dropping musical moments on *XO*, a swirling piano solo that combines the melodic strength of Smith's vocal with the rhythmic intensity of his guitar part; flawlessly transposed, as Smith was given to doing, for the particular timbre and rhythmic response of the piano. Schnapf and Rothrock's sonic treatment suits the song perfectly: a storm in a teacup, at once cathartic and heartbreakingly muted.

According to both Crane and Schnapf, "Pitseleh" is one of the songs on *XO* that seemed to emerge out of nowhere in the studio, with no demos or live performances preexisting its recording. Smith never talked much about "Pitseleh" in interviews, and rarely performed it. Some recall hearing him say that it was "too long and boring," or that it was a "lyrics-based song" which he didn't feel translated well live. The more romantic interpretation of these facts is that Smith held the song to be of particular personal significance. The less romantic (and, considering Smith's practical attitudes toward creativity, more likely) interpretation is that, given the lack of revision the song saw before it was recorded, Smith felt that the song was musically undercooked.

"Independence Day"

"Independence Day" was the last song recorded for *XO*, the product of a later session that was intended to

provide b-sides for the record's singles. Aesthetically,
the obvious difference between "Independence Day"
and the rest of *XO* is its reliance upon a drum loop,
credited in the album's liners to co-producer Tom
Rothrock. In a sense, the loop proves to be an interesting challenge for Smith—while many of the songs on
XO depend on percussion to articulate their structural
arcs (or operate nimbly within the structural absences
afforded by a lack of percussion), "Independence Day"
relies primarily on chord changes and subtle layering
to give the song its shape.

"Independence Day" is at its strongest before
the drum loop even begins. Smith had a knack
for writing acoustic guitar intros that masterfully
foreshadow the overall feel and arc of a song ("The
Ballad of Big Nothing" from *Either/Or* stands out
in this regard), and "Independence Day" opens with
one of his finest. Coming out of "Pitseleh," the
opening bars of "Independence Day" seem intentionally vague and transitory, hinting at a transfor-
mation without revealing its end result (mirroring
the lyrical image of a "future butterfly"). When the
vocal melody from the song's chorus materializes,
it becomes clear that we have left the hushed intro-
spection of "Pitseleh;" we have emerged into day-
light (where we will remain for both "Independence
Day" and "Bled White").

Given its last-minute creation, "Independence Day" is perhaps not as lyrically developed as the rest of *XO*; the rhyming of "today" with "day," and "ooh" with "you" are the kind of lyrical fallbacks that Smith tended to excise when revising his work. That said, "Independence Day" is a welcome addition to the album's flow; a laid-back and fairly optimistic song sandwiched between the wrenching "Pitseleh" and the defiant "Bled White."

"Bled White"

Originally entitled "Crush Blind" and then "Poor White," "Bled White" has a rich and illuminating history. The song was recorded twice at Jackpot!: once on 8-track and once on 16-track. The earlier of these two recordings (then called "Crush Blind") is the most markedly different; while the song's chords and melody are as they will later appear, the song is accompanied by an unmemorable monophonic keyboard line (played, according to Crane, on a Hammond L102 organ), and does not have the call and response vocals that make its verses so lively and dynamic.

The lyrical reworking of "Bled White" is among Smith's most thorough and skillful. In its earliest incarnations, the bridge of "Bled White" presents us with a series of observations and references, both general and specific:

> Who's the girl with the blank expression?
> Everyone's trying to put someone to shame.
> But happiness pulls you the other direction,
> Going to Pioneer Square to watch it rain.

The association of "happiness" and "watching it rain" seems at once too easy and too heavy-handed to meet Smith's rigorous standards. In a slightly later live version (from March of 1997), this line has been rewritten:

> Who's the girl with the blank expression?
> Everyone's looking for someone they can blame.
> But happiness pulls me in my direction,
> Going to Pioneer Square to find your name.

As with many early incarnations of Smith's lyrics, this intermediate version of the bridge reads like an evocative yet disconnected sequence of isolated lines. It is only when the recording of *XO* is already well underway that the final version of the bridge begins to take shape:

> Here he comes with the blank expression
> Especially for me 'cause he knows I feel the same
> 'Cause happy and sad come in quick succession
> I'm never going to become what you became

As in many of Smith's lyrics, the bridge of "Bled White" is host to a remarkably complex play of subjects. Here *he* comes with the blank expression, "especially" (implying the presence—if not physical—of others as well) for *me* because he knows that *I* share the feeling behind that expression. "I'm never going to become what you became" is a remarkably bold and assured line, bolstered and contextualized by the newfound narrative continuity of the bridge. When the snare drum picks up at the line's end, you can almost see Smith confidently trotting off from the encounter that he has just described with his inimitable combination of emotional specificity and situational vagueness.

The verse immediately following the bridge is telling as well:

> Don't you dare disturb me
> (Don't complicate my peace of mind)
>   While I'm balancing my past
> (Don't complicate my peace of mind)
> 'Cause you can't help or hurt me
> (Faith in me, baby's just a waste of time)
> Like it already has
> I may not seem quite right
> But I'm not fucked, not quite

This verse treads familiar thematic ground, describing the precariousness of the past, and how the attempt to "balance" that past can leave beyond help or harm from others (again, the "airless cell"). Just as the song's bridge grew bolder and more confident, the final line of this verse grew more optimistic—in the song's earliest demo, Smith sang "if you think I'm fucked, you're right."

Interestingly, Crane recalls that the response vocals as they appeared on *XO* were written last-minute while Smith was already well into recording at Sunset. Extant demos and live recordings seem to support this; in the second studio demo of "Bled White," Smith simply repeats "white city on the 409," and response vocals are entirely absent from every live performance of "Bled White" through the recording of *XO*. The use of the phrase "waste of time" to end multiple lines, and the repetition of "white city on the yellow line" in the song's first and second verses seem a bit sloppy and arbitrary given the meticulous specificity of the song's lead vocal. But this slight air of randomness succeeds in giving these lines a different voice, enhancing the song's call-and-response structure.

Along with "Independence Day," "Bled White" is one of the most upbeat songs on *XO*. Blackness and darkness permeate the record and while, according to Crane, the lack of color in "Bled White" has its origins in Smith's skeptical eye toward gentrification, it ultimately casts "Bled White" as one of

XO's few daytime songs. If blackness is the place where the writer isolates himself, "Bled White" the song of a "color reporter," walking around a city and taking it in. Notably, it is the only song on *XO* where action and observation seem concurrent, perhaps because it is a song rooted in the *action* of observing.

"Bled White" is one of two songs on *XO* on which Smith did not play drums. According to Schnapf, Smith was having trouble getting the feel of the song just right, and opted to enlist sometimes-Beck drummer Joey Waronker (son of DreamWorks exec Lenny, and original drummer for the mighty Walt Mink) instead. Smith was without a doubt a capable drummer, but his particular style was more steady and "heavy" than nimble and propulsive—on "Waltz #2," you can almost *feel* the bulk of the drum sticks. "Bled White" and "Bottle Up and Explode" are the only two songs on *XO* in which the drum part is not rhythmically anticipated by another instrument, be it bass, guitar or piano—in effect, the only two songs where Smith's style of drumming would fail to drive the song forward as needed. Though Smith wrote "Bled White" and played drums on multiple demo recordings, he was ultimately able to distance the song itself from his own role in creating it, and to work—as always—in the service of the former.

"Waltz #1"

According to Crane, "Waltz #1" was temporarily titled "Bushmill's," "[having] more to do with a hangover than anything." As such, the song's placement on *XO* is apt; a hazy, disoriented comedown after the propulsive and tightly wound "Bled White."

An early version of "Waltz #1," recorded by Crane at Jackpot!, has been frequently circulated as a b-side and a compilation track. Musically, it is very similar to the version recorded for *XO*. Its lyrics are host to only a handful of notable changes, the first of which occurs midway through the song. ("Waltz #1" does not really have "verses" or "choruses" to speak of.) In the Jackpot! recording, Smith sings:

> I thought you knew
> Now I take it from the top and make
>   the repetition stop
> It never ever went away

On *XO*, the first two lines are combined:

> Going through every out I used to cop to make
>   the repetition stop
> What was I supposed to say?

In both cases, Smith cleverly intones "repetition stop" at the very moment when the song's repeating musical figure momentarily subsides. Smith's revision of the verse highlights the brief silence that follows it; "what was I supposed to say?" omits both the lyric that downplays the previous line's cleverness (for a moment the musical repetition did, in fact, go away) and the awkward pickup syllable "it."

The second notable change occurs immediately after the break. In the Jackpot! version, Smith sings "now I'm scared to leave my zone—we're both alone—I'm coming home." On *XO*, the line becomes "Now I never leave my zone—we're both alone—I'm going home." (The "zone" in "Waltz #1" parallels the "place where I make no mistakes" in "Waltz #2," and "the safety of a pitch-black mind" in "Oh Well, Okay.") The change from "coming home" to "going home" speaks to the precision of Smith's word choice; one slight directional shift substantially alters the sense of place conjured by the song as a whole. "Coming home" implies that the person you're addressing is already there; "going home" removes that implicit third party and its resultant sense of connection and groundedness, reinforcing the free-floating and amorphous feel of the song itself.

Notably, "Waltz #1" is the only song on *XO* that fades out; the "repetition," it turns out, doesn't stop after all.

"Amity"

Like "Baby Britain," "Amity" was mostly tracked at Jackpot!, engineered by Larry Crane. It is by far the most "lo-fi" song on *XO*. According to Crane, there was a problematic degree of bleed in the drum microphones; to remedy this, Schnapf and Rothrock created a sample of the snare drum from a part of the song where Smith plays primarily on the ride cymbal, then triggered this sample during the parts of the song where the hi-hat was problematically loud in the snare mic.

In the *Big Takeover* interview, Smith describes "Amity" not as a love song, but rather as a sort of self-examination brought about by the presence of another:

> It's a really unguarded song—I made up the lyrics in a couple of minutes and didn't change them. I like the way it feels, although it's not an especially deep song at all. It's, I don't know . . . just a big rock song. It's a pretty simple song. It's not so much about the words themselves, but more about how the whole thing sounds. Some friends of mine said it sounded like I was trying to get something romantic going with someone, and that's not what it was supposed to be about. It was supposed to be, "you're really fun to be with and I really like you a lot because of that, but I am really, really depressed." But I don't know if

that came across. When I said, "ready to go," it was supposed to mean tired of living. . . . I was saying, "I really like you and it's really great to hang out with someone who is happy and easy-going, but I don't feel like that and I can't be with you."

The spontaneity of "Amity" is evident from the almost-hypnotic repetition of its subject's name that opens the song. "Amity" is host to some of the most contrived and unrefined lines in Smith's oeuvre; "God don't make no junk," "'Cause you laugh and talk, and 'cause you make my world rock"—but this is no accident. Throughout "Amity," Smith sounds almost drunk on the presence of the song's subject. His openness and exuberance, expressed in part through the very absence of his characteristic precision—are what make the song so compelling and infectious.

. . . That is, until the song's sobering final line; a comedown in which "good to go" (a line that, to my ears, reveals none of the fatalism that Smith intended) is appended with the word "home." The giddy drunkenness of "Amity" ends the same as the disoriented drunkenness of "Waltz #1"; going home, alone. If Smith intended for "ready to go" to mean "ready to die," he effectively undermined himself by casting the song's final moment as such a dramatic downturn.

Even the spontaneous and urgent "Amity" was masterfully enhanced and honed during the mixing of *XO*. In an earlier mix consisting entirely of tracks from the Jackpot! session, the squalling electric guitar note ringing out over the second half of the song's second verse is mixed noticeably louder, enhancing the song's texture but ultimately distracting from Smith's vocal. Similarly, the song's verses originally contained prominent vocal harmonies by Smith and friend/collaborator Pete Krebs on the lines "open all the time" and "make my world rock," very pleasant in their own right but ultimately disruptive to the song's immersive effect, calling attention to its artifice and creating a sense of distance from Smith's absorbing lead vocal. At Sunset, Smith and Krebs' harmonies were reworked and rerecorded much more subtly by Smith himself, the bass part from the Jackpot! session was retracked, and understated strings were added into the mix. Even as Smith was given greater means to record, he remained remarkably sensitive to how sonically pleasing studio flourishes could work against a song's nature; the process of arranging *XO* was hardly just one of piling on.

"Oh Well, Okay"

Aside from "Independence Day," "Oh Well, Okay" appears to be the last song Smith completed for *XO*, having demoed the song with Crane at Jackpot! on March 31, 1998. In an interview with *Interview* magazine, Smith described the song as his favorite on the record, for that very reason:

> My favorite is the newest one, since I haven't heard it as many times as some of the others. It's called "Oh Well, Okay." It's slow and quiet and sort of describes a silhouette of someone. It would sound ridiculous to talk about it too much, but essentially it's about how a silhouette is permanently turned away from you. The person is being described as if they were this photograph. And they weren't always turned away from me, but now they are and they seem to stay like that. It's kind of a sad song.

Smith introduces this "photograph" in the song's second verse:

> I got pictures, I just don't see it anymore
> Climbing hour upon hour through a total bore
> With the one I keep where it never fades
> In the safety of a pitch black mind
> An airless cell that blocks the day

The use of plural "pictures" and the singular "it" makes it clear that it is not the pictures themselves that Smith can no longer see; as in "Sweet Adeline," pictures cannot fully stand in for that which they represent. Here, once again, the future—in which the picture threatens to fade—is figured as dangerous and threatening, combated as in "Tomorrow, Tomorrow" by the negation of the present. (That fear of the future is itself predicated upon a need to preserve the past, even as a memento of the past fails to capture its subject.) "Climbing hour upon hour through a total bore" is a great example of Smith's tendency to spatialize emotional conceits, and of his lyrical precision: to bore is the opposite of to climb.

As with "Pitseleh," "Oh Well, Okay" is host to an instrumental solo that subtly but powerfully refigures its vocal melody. In this case, it is a hazy slide guitar solo, which injects a physically palpable pause into the vocal melody Smith sings as "always turned away" and "see it anymore." One of Smith's greatest talents as an instrumentalist was his ability to write guitar parts that seem to *breathe*; unencumbered by words, Smith's guitar transforms the melody of "Oh Well, Okay" into the heavy sigh of its title.

"Bottle Up and Explode!"

Though Heatmiser recorded numerous times at pro studios in Portland, an early version of "Bottle Up and Explode!" is among the first of Smith's solo songs to be tracked in a professional recording environment, the product of a session with Greg Di Gesu at Waterfront Studios in Hoboken, New Jersey on March 25 and 26, 1996. Di Gesu recalls how Smith carried over the methodology he developed recording at home:

> [Waterfront] was a reputable studio, and I think it was different from the approaches he had been doing when he was recording at home. He was doing all the parts here too, tracking vocals, adding drums, two or three guitar tracks, bass. But I think ultimately he was still transitioning to that kind of a situation. He came out on publishing money, and we had a really really good time and a good connection together. But I think there's a certain apprehension in the record-ings, in the performance. When we worked together, he worked. He would get his guitar part, listen back, make sure everything was ok, then he'd do the second part. Keith, my assistant engineer at the time, called today, and he reminded me of some good things: he remembers that Elliott would want me to put rough mixes on cassette, and he'd put them on his Walkman. The studio sat on a river, and he'd go out there, smoke cigarettes, and listen to the stuff. It seemed like he used the methodology that he had used in the past, where he knows what worked for him. But I still think that being in a control room with a huge Trident A Range [mixing board] was very different for him.

In the version of "Bottle Up and Explode!" recorded by Di Gesu, Smith's guitar is tuned down and—as Di Gesu suggests—his vocal performance uncertain. The resultant recording is at once sweeter and more ominous than the version that made it onto *XO*. Ultimately, though, the decision to transpose "Bottle Up and Explode!" to a higher key suited the song well; the song of Smith's voice edging up toward the top of his range better evokes the emotional dynamic of the song's title.

As one of the older songs on *XO*, "Bottle Up and Explode" went through a series of interesting lyrical changes. The version recorded by Di Gesu, and concurrent live versions, demonstrate a marked difference in the song's second verse:

> She looks at him like he's never known her—
> It's only been a year and half.
> Thinking that that was a matter of fact.
> Thinking that he was about to come over,
> I've been standing up waiting for you—you
> never showed.

By November of 1997, the opening lyrics of the verse have been altered:

> You look at him like you don't want to know him,
> But I know in the past that you have.

The opening of two concurrent lines with the words "thinking that" is the type of repetition that Smith tended to edit out when revising his work. On the final version of *XO*, the verse has changed substantially from its original form:

> You look at him like you've never known him,
> But I know for a fact that you have.
> The last time you cried who'd you think was inside?
> Thinking that you were about to come over,
> But I'm tired now of waiting for you—you
>   never show.

In his review of *XO*, John Darnielle—a tremendously accomplished lyricist in his own right—eloquently described the unassuming brilliance of this verse:

> One of my favorite lines in the song goes: "You look at him like you've never known him/ But I know for a fact that you have." It's the line that leads off the song's second verse, coming out of nowhere at all. The first verse had been a solitary affair uncluttered by second parties. You and I both know the sentiment behind such a line; it requires no explication. The acrid taste it leaves in your mouth speaks for itself. What's unusual here is that since the feeling behind such a line is self-evident, its author offers no narrative detail of any kind to flesh it out for you. The song is a laundry list of words and phrases that prick at very specific emotional centers, but which add up to virtually nothing—they are like a dream of a song

rather than an actual song. . . . To find such painterly writing framed by the pleasant, palatable music that we find here is nothing short of alarming.

Similarly, Smith's description of the colors "red, white, blue" is intentionally presented without narrative context. In the *Big Takeover* interview, Smith described how this line was specifically meant to trigger the listener's imagination:

> I was thinking about fireworks exploding. It could be a celebration, but then again, it could be something bad. I just try and make connections between things. I'm not so interested in telling complete stories anymore—now I like it better if the songs are like abstract movies. . . . The song won't complete itself without someone activating their imagination. The music is supposed to do that. A lot of my favorite songs are ones that aren't complete without me finishing them in my head.

Here, Smith summarizes why it can be so hard to say what exactly his songs are "about" even as, in Darnielle's words, they "prick at very specific emotional centers." The closing lines of "Bottle Up and Explode!"—"I'll make it outside / I'll get through becoming you"— operate on a similar principle; we never learn who "you" refers to, but the way Smith repeats "becoming you" over the song's coda requires no explanation.

"A Question Mark"

In a video interview for Musician.com, Smith describes his songwriting as follows: "I don't really think about it in terms of language, I think about it more like shapes." He then goes on to play "A Question Mark"; a perfect fit, seeing as the song's spare opening notes seem to paint that very punctuation mark. In that same interview, Smith goes on to say "I'm really into chord changes. That was the thing I liked when I was a kid. So I'm not like a . . . I don't make up a 'riff' really. It's usually like . . . That sequence has some implied melody in it or something like that."

"A Question Mark" proves exemplary in this respect; the chord voicings in its verse contain almost all of the song's melodic turns, several of which actually get subsumed by a bass saxophone part in version recorded for *XO*. The decision to prominently feature the bass saxophone (and to include an unaccompanied snippet of it at the end of "Bottle up and Explode!") makes for a substantial and welcome textural shift in the flow of *XO*, but obscures some of "A Question Mark"'s innate musical logic. The instrumental demo of "A Question Mark," recorded by Crane at Jackpot on January 13, 1998, places the horn part (played on guitar) farther back in the mix, allowing more room for the major 3rds in Smith's nimble guitar part to sketch the song's basic melody.

"A Question Mark" not only restates Smith's belief in uncertainty, but also associates the illusion of certainty with "hatred." Smith wrote many songs that suggest that, in the words of Larry Crane, "things that you think are one way . . . are actually another way." "A Question Mark" is Smith's "things that you think are one way can't be simplified to any one way at all" song:

> I've got a question mark
> You've got a need to always take some shot in the dark
> I don't have to make pretend the picture I'm in is
>   totally clear
> You think that all things have a way they ought
>   to appear
> 'Cause you know, you know, you know, you know
> You know, I don't, I dream
> Don't know what you mean

The end of the song's second verse lays out the dangers of the causal mindset Smith implicitly rejects in "Pitseleh":

> You're giving back a little hatred now to the world
> 'Cause it treated you bad
> 'Cause you couldn't keep the great unknown from
>   making you mad

Here, the attempt to fix meaning is seen as a vengeful act; an outlook that seems to inform Smith's lyrics in approach as well as content. As with many songs on *XO*, "A Question Mark" reveals much of its hand during its bridge, in which the song finally resolves to the G major chord it has been hinting at since its first notes:

> Said your final word, but honesty and love could've
>   kept us together
> One day you'll see it's worth it after all
> If you ever want to say you're sorry you can
>   give me a call

Notably, this is the only time on the record that the word "sorry" appears. Not only is Smith himself *not* the one apologizing—the apology is only invited, not offered or stated. In Smith's lyrical world, hubristic certainty is the only thing that seems to warrant an apology, and that apology (requested somewhat playfully during the song's most upbeat passage) doesn't seem to count for much. Real emotional harm like that described in "Pitseleh" evades such simple solutions.

The bridge of "A Question Mark" is, as with many of Smith's more slyly uplifting moments, philosophically optimistic even while it addresses a personal failure. The simple nihilism sometimes attributed to Smith's work is overstated and misleading; for all of the doubt Smith directs both inward and outward, he is not an advocate of sheer hopelessness. In Smith's songs, people routinely fail to live up to the betterment they wish for themselves, or cannot accept the love that is offered to them. But the concepts of betterment and love are not debased, dismissed or destroyed—just difficult.

"Everybody Cares, Everybody Understands"

Though it didn't surface in Smith's live repertoire until 1997, "Everybody Cares, Everybody Understands" is actually one of the oldest songs on *XO*, its basic musical underpinnings dating back to Harum Scarum, a band that Smith was in with Tony Lash before the two played together in Heatmiser. (Harum Scarum had also worked on a version of "Sweet Adeline" with different lyrics.)

The subject matter that inspired the final version of "Everybody Cares, Everybody Understands" is well documented, and does not bear too much elaborating here. Before the recording of *XO*, Smith briefly stayed at a rehab center in Arizona, and was none too pleased with the people responsible for sending him there, nor with the experience itself.

Larry Crane has a distinct memory of hearing a rough mix of "Everybody Cares" and being taken aback by how specifically pointed its lyrics were:

> I went down for about a week to LA, and hung out with
> Tom and Rob and Elliott at Sunset Sound as sessions
> for *XO* were happening. And the first thing [Elliott]
> did was, he picked me up at the airport, and he said
> "here's something we're working on," and he played
> me "Everybody Cares, Everybody Understands" and
> I thought "that's mean." And I knew what it was about
> and it was like, "ooh, wow." And there was even a line
> that was slightly different, that was even more direct to
> the person it was about. And I was like "oh man, that's
> pretty tough. You're gonna put that on the record?"

This early mix of "Everybody Cares" has long leaked
to the Internet, and indeed its lyrics do indeed allude
more directly to Smith's stay in Arizona:

> Everybody cares, everybody understands—
> Yes, everybody cares about you—as a matter of fact
>   I'm sure they do.
> But if you don't act just right, they kick you in the head.
> But I wouldn't take it offensively—they're doing
>   it out of sympathy,
> And you're the one who's bringing it all about.
>
> So here I lay dreaming, looking at the brilliant sun
> Raining its guiding light upon everyone
>
> For a moment's rest I leaned against the banister
> After running upstairs again and again from a place
>   you people, you've never been,

With all of Fear City's finest following behind
Who with the greatest skill and resourcefulness,
   after putting me under a wrongful arrest,
Stepped me out to the desert to dry and die

Here I lay dreaming, looking at the brilliant sun
Pushing it's guiding light upon everyone

The dream-killing doctor says to describe my dream.
But some things are for no one to know and for you,
   twelve-stepping cop, to not find out.

Ultimately, via what Schnapf calls a "last-minute change of heart," Smith revised these lyrics. But Smith's final revisions, though less narratively and geographically specific, certainly don't dull the song's sharp edges. As with many of Smith's songs, "Everybody Cares" gets more emotionally pointed as it veers *away* from personal specificity. The final version of the song's closing line: "You say you mean well, you don't know what you mean / You fucking ought to stay the hell away from things you know nothing about" is one of the most direct and stinging on all of *XO*, encapsulating Smith's disdain for self-serving good will and unfounded certainty alike.

Similarly, the song's opening verse becomes more pointed in its final iteration:

Everybody cares, everybody understands—
Yes, everybody cares about you, yeah, and whether
   or not you want them to.

It's a chemical embrace that kicks you
    in the head
To a pure synthetic sympathy that infuriates
    you totally
And a quiet lie that makes you wanna scream
    and shout.

"A chemical embrace that kicks you in the head" is a prime example of Smith's use of substance abuse imagery to describe a force (like a romantic "embrace") that overrides intellect and rational thought. The language of chemical dependence is also implied in the wonderfully alliterative phrase "pure synthetic sympathy." Similarly, Smith's use of the word "pushing" in every performance of "Everybody Cares" prior to its final recording is a thought-provoking recontextualization of drug abuse terminology. But while the idea of the sun as a "pusher" is intriguing, it ultimately seems incongruous with *XO* at large. Throughout the album, the sun is often presented as a figure whose light threatens to penetrate the "endless cell that blocks the day," that reoccurring place of safety and isolation that is, itself, associated with drug use (even when—as in *XO* outtake "New Monkey"—it is also positioned as a place of creativity.) When a "fully loaded" Smith "[stares] down the sun" in "Sweet Adeline," it is not the sun that is rendering him "deaf and dumb and done."

The finale of "Everybody Cares" is the most instrumentally dense portion of *XO*, building layer upon layer of what Schnapf calls "sprinkles," including keyboard work by Smith's friend and collaborator Jon Brion. It is a deft musical literalization of the song's conceit; immediately following Smith's warning to "stay the hell way," here is "everybody," a dizzying array of instrumental voices that grows overbearing and menacing as it builds.

"I Didn't Understand"

In the earliest live versions of the "I Didn't Understand", Smith sings over a characteristically spindly acoustic guitar part. In a preliminary recording of the song, widely circulated among fans on the "Jackpot Sessions" compilation, Smith accompanies himself on piano. For *XO*, Smith ran with an idea of Schnapf's, born of repeat listens to the Beach Boys' *Pet Sounds Sessions* box set:

> I was listening to a lot of Beach Boys, and I heard a lot of a capella versions. And so I just said, "what if you did that?" And that was it. I just planted that one little seed. And then he did a version, and he basically played it on piano, on the [Roland digital multitrack] VS880. He basically picked apart the piano chord and harmonized it, and came up with that big

4 part-or-more version. And we listened to it, and thought, "huh, that's really cool, but it's a bit too . . . liturgical." And he went back and just did a different version. And we also did a different version where we took that and just added strings to it.

The earliest studio recording of "I Didn't Understand" (then called "Watch the Worlds Collide") has markedly different lyrics from the version that closes *XO*:

> Everybody's looking for the next in line to love
> Then ignore, put out, and put away
> And I'd be happy just to be relieved from duty
>   right away—
> I know what's gonna happen to me
> When people talk about love,
> They're painting pictures of someone's pretty side
> But go look yourself in the face
> And watch the worlds collide, watch
>   the worlds collide
>
> Waiting for a bus to take my thoughts away from us
> And drop me off far away from you
> 'Cause my feelings never change a bit—I'm waiting
>   to get over it
> But I know what it is I have to do
> When people talk about love
> They're painting pictures of someone's pretty side
> But I look myself in the face, and watch the worlds
>   collide, watch the worlds collide

In a slightly later live version (performed on July 29, 1997), Smith's lyrics have begun to resemble their final form, save for the song's closing stanza:

> So don't talk to me about love
> Or paint me pictures of my one pretty side
> When you've seen us both in my face,
> Watch the worlds collide, watch the worlds collide

The theme of intra-personal rupture and unification is one that Smith addresses in many songs, including "Cecilia/Amanda" and, perhaps most memorably, post-*Either/Or* single "Division Day." Ultimately, though, these lyrical themes faded from "I Didn't Understand" (though they are beautifully rendered on *XO*, as Smith's unaccompanied, multitracked vocals finally join in unison at the song's end). By November of 1997, Smith was performing the song with what would be the final revision of its closing words:

> You once talked to me about love
> And you painted pictures of a Neverneverland
> And I could have gone to that place
> But I didn't understand, I didn't understand,
> I didn't understand

Smith finishes *XO* as he began it: with a picture. This time, the picture is not of the lyrically ubiquitous "you and me," but rather of the quite unexpected "Neverneverland." In J. M. Barrie's original *Peter Pan*, we are given a clue as to why this fictional place might be relevant to Smith:

> I don't know whether you have ever seen a map of a person's mind. Doctors sometimes draw maps of other parts of you, and your own map can become intensely interesting, but catch them trying to draw a map of a child's mind, which is not only confused, but keeps going round all the time. There are zigzag lines on it, just like your temperature on a card, and these are probably roads in the island, for the Neverland is always more or less an island, with astonishing splashes of colour here and there, and coral reefs and rakish-looking craft in the offing, and savages and lonely lairs, and gnomes who are mostly tailors, and caves through which a river runs, and princes with six elder brothers, and a hut fast going to decay, and one very small old lady with a hooked nose. It would be an easy map if that were all, but there is also first day at school, religion, fathers, the round pond, needle-work, murders, hangings, verbs that take the dative, chocolate pudding day, getting into braces, say ninety-nine, three-pence for pulling out your tooth yourself, and so on, and either these are part of the island or they are another map showing through, and it is all rather confusing, especially as nothing will stand still.

Here, Barrie describes "Neverland" *not* just as a place where you never grow up, but rather as a place where your imagination dictates reality; a world forged of the mind that is not "pitch-black" but rather enlivened by "astonishing splashes of color." Furthermore, Barrie's "Neverland" is not a simple utopia, nor is it a place of unbridled escapism. Like a child's imagination, it is populated by both the mundane and the fantastical; the beautiful and the grotesque. It is an imaginary world haunted by reality.

Perhaps, then, Smith's assertion that he "could have gone to that place" isn't all that far-fetched. After all, Neverneverland is a place accessed not by knowledge, but by *belief*. It is "wonderful, lovely thoughts," and the magical dust of a fairy, that grants you flight to Neverland. And, as Peter tells Wendy, a lack of belief not only closes off Neverland, it literally *kills* the magical beings who take you there: "Every time a child says, 'I don't believe in fairies,' there is a fairy somewhere that falls down dead." If we picture love as a Neverneverland, then perhaps it, too, is something that can only exist if we believe in it. Indeed, for all the sadness expressed on *XO*, there is just as strong a pull against it. "I'm not half what I wish I was." "You've got a look in your eye when you're saying goodbye, like you want to say hi." Darkness is inescapable on *XO*, but it is not valued.

In an August 1998 interview with *Well Rounded Entertainment*, Smith repeated a line he gave in many interviews to counter his image as a "sad sack": "If there was one kind of song I wish I could write it would be more like 'I Second That Emotion,' by Smokey Robinson than like some really dark, depressing song." In a strange way, Smith both addresses and enacts his wish with "I Didn't Understand." While the song is not triumphant—Smith *didn't* go to that place—he *does* understand, now, that it is not impossible. Knowledge and certainty are eviscerated on *XO*, but Smith leaves us with a potent parting gift: belief.

Discussing which tracks were "relevant" to *XO* proves difficult given Smith's way of working; songs would frequently be abandoned, recycled, and reapproached later. For the sake of casting a net that is not too wide, I am only discussing songs that were originally slated for inclusion on *XO*, and "Miss Misery," a song that is inexorably tied to this period in Smith's career.

"Cecilia/Amanda" [Unreleased]

In looking through a prolific artist's rarities, songs like "Cecilia/Amanda" are true treasures; beautiful, illustrative songs never completed for release but somehow made more precious by their obscurity.

Though "Cecilia/Amanda" was originally slated for inclusion on *XO*, Schnapf suggests that Smith never finished it to his own satisfaction:

> I don't think that song was really gonna come to
> be. . . . It was a really old song that had been kicking
> around forever. . . . It was something he was trying to
> rework, and it never quite got there. It's an old song
> that I think he had written with a friend of his who's
> now a doctor.

That friend is Garrick Duckler, who played with
Smith in his high school band Stranger Than Fiction
and later co-wrote a cassette's worth of songs with
Smith under the name A Murder of Crows. Only one
of Duckler's collaborations with Smith has been formally released—"Night Cap" from Heatmiser's *Cop
and Speeder* record—but Smith did occasionally use
a snippet or idea from Duckler's music, or in some
cases put an entire set of Duckler's lyrics to his own
music.

Duckler was kind enough to offer some of his
recollections of "Cecilia/Amanda":

> It was [originally] "Celia said to Amanda" not one
> name "Cecilia-Amanda," [but] actually he did change
> it to "Cecilia/Amanda," which is funny because I
> remember that Elliott was joking with me that Celia
> is not really a woman's name but is the stuff in your
> lungs and then I told him that the song is really about
> microscopic parts of the lungs trying to sort out their

problems. We'd joke around a lot like this. He had a
wonderful sense of humor.

"Cecilia/Amanda" is a favorite among Smith's fans,
and with good cause. Musically, it is one of the most
elegant songs in Smith's repertoire, released or unre-
leased. The only extant studio version of "Cecilia/
Amanda" was recorded at Jackpot!, but a new recording was approached and subsequently abandoned
during the *XO* sessions at Sunset Sound. According
to Schnapf, the "b-list" string section hired to per-
form on *XO* (with the exception of ex-Mahavishnu
Orchestra violinist Jerrod "Jerry" Goodman) struggled with the bent note that Smith performed on a
synthesizer for the Jackpot! demo:

> There were big scoring dates that day, all the really
> good players were scattered through all the big film
> studios. It ended up being ok, but there were certain
> things they could not do. They couldn't swing at all.

The skill of the string players notwithstanding, it is hard
to imagine a perfect organic realization of the synthe-
sized string bend on the one extant studio recording of
"Cecilia/Amanda." Though the sound quality is less than
stellar, the Jackpot! demo of "Cecilia/Amanda" presents a full arrangement much in the vein of "Waltz #2"
or "baby Britain," replete with piano, guitar, bass

(courtesy of Quasi's Sam Coomes) and drums. Lyrically, "Cecilia/Amanda" can be read as a more philosophically adventurous counterpoint to "Baby Britain"—an incisive character sketch of a person who fails to live up to her potential. In "Cecilia/Amanda," Smith's interest in personal rupture is given a literal manifestation in the form of a mother and child.

Smith closes "Cecilia/Amanda" with a play at contrasts:

> Amanda put on a new party dress yesterday
> Dancing to a record you scratched
> Some deal in amateur acting, making opposites match

This final line appears in earlier versions as "the two of you's a study in making total opposites match." The equation of "making opposites match" and "amateur acting" speaks to the clumsy impossibility of uniting opposites. In an earlier verse, Smith describes a strip club (where the mother works as a "pretty dancer") as "a place where lonely men pay to make their opposites match," casting an air of sleaze and desperation on the very (impossible) idea of reconciling opposites. Opposing ideas can coexist—and often do in Smith's lyrics—but they can never match.

Though it is among his most philosophically provocative songs, I suspect that Smith never fine-tuned the lyrics of "Cecilia/Amanda" to his satisfaction. The end of the song's second verse was refined numerous times, but even the lyrics on the Jackpot! recording seem to fall short of Smith's standards:

> Every remembrance of you has been buried below
> Every memory that I unhappily know

The themes are familiar, but the language (especially the parallel use of "remembrance" and "memory") is unusually clunky. This seems to be the couplet in the song that Smith struggled with the most; in the earliest live version of the song, Smith sang "She ain't got a father now 'cause he's buried below / Way up high in the sky with all the people she knows." Given Smith's tendency to abandon and reapproach songs, there does exist a chance that "Cecilia/Amanda" might have been picked up and completed for another album. As it stands, "Cecilia/Amanda" is a poignant realization of Smith's attitude toward potential, its very incompleteness testifying to the vastness of Smith's talent.

New Monkey [Released on *New Moon*]

"New Monkey" is one of a handful of Smith's songs that explicitly utilizes the language of drug abuse to broach broader philosophical and emotional issues.

Smith begins the song by introducing a "sidewalk boss," who sees Smith as a "picture of dissatisfaction that he can only see as a junkie." Smith continues, "though I might be straight as an arrow, he's busy shaking hands with my monkey."

Here, the familiar metaphor of a monkey on one's back is extended beyond its common association with chemical addiction. What, exactly, is the proverbial monkey on Smith's back? It isn't entirely clear. The song's chorus—"anything is better than nothing"—suggests that this vagary is not unintentional; Smith applies the language of addiction to any behavior that goes against reason, be it substance abuse, self-destruction, or ill-advised romantic pursuits. The last verse of "New Monkey" is more specific in its unexpected allusion to the songwriting process:

> I'm here with my cup, afraid to look up
> This is how I spend my time
> Lazing around, head hanging down
> Stuck inside my imagination
> Busy making something from nothing
> Pictures of hope and depression
> Anything is better than nothing

Here, the split between the act of songwriting and the life of the writer is made explicit; Smith is "stuck" inside his imagination, but he is "making something from nothing" (given Smith's tendency toward self-deprecation in his lyrics, "nothing" may very well be a reference to the singer himself). Similarly, "something"—"pictures of hope and depression"—can be read as Smith's own songs. Thus, the place of fearful stasis articulated throughout *XO* is also figured as a haven for writerly creativity. It's an oddly unromantic vision of songwriting that seems in keeping with Smith's workmanlike approach to the creative process. Songwriting, like anything else, is something to do—and it's a lot better than some of its alternatives.

"Memory Lane" [Released on *From a Basement on the Hill*]

"Memory Lane" was officially released on 2004's posthumous *From a Basement on the Hill*, but the song was originally slated for inclusion on *XO*. Thematically, it is a handy summation of Smith's suspect view of memory and the past. It is also a particularly elegant example of Smith's tendency to spatialize or literalize common metaphors; in this case, "memory lane" is reimagined as "the place you end up when you lose the chase." A live version of the song from October 1997 offers some interesting glimpses into Smith's lyrical concerns at the time of *XO*:

This is the place you end up when you lose
    the chase,
Where the passion and the pill make you
    easier to kill.
And all anybody knows is you look messed up—
They inspect you in the head and send you
    back to bed.

Isolation draws into its static, into night, builds
    a little house for you to stay.
But everybody's scared of this place,
    staying away—
No one comes here, Memory Lane.

It's just the appearance everybody fears,
Just to see you try to get a very abrasive
    piece of it,
What they never knew 'cause they did not want to.
You keep the doors and windows shut and never
    show a soul again.

But isolation draws into a static, into night, builds
    a little house for you to stay.
But everybody's scared of this place, staying away—
No one comes here, Memory Lane.
If it's your decision to be open about yourself, be
    careful or else—you better be careful or else.

I'm uncomfortable apart—it's all written
    on my chart.
And I take what's given me, most cooperatively.

I do what people say and lie in bed all day,
But I'm never going to cry under the doctor's eye.

In a January 14, 1998 performance, "Memory
Lane"'s second verse covers similar ground:

It's here a prickly fear will eventually appear
With a mountain of cliché that it dumps
    right in your way.
Everyone took it for true 'cause they did
    not know you.
You'll keep the doors and windows shut and swear
    you'll never show a soul again.

This verse is thematically related to the song's bridge,
which remains constant over the five or so years that
Smith worked on the song: "If it's your decision to be
open about yourself, be careful or else." Openness is
an invitation to being misunderstood, and the effects
of that misunderstanding (as in "Everybody Cares")
can be devastating.

The original chorus of "Memory Lane" ties
together many of the lyrical figures from *XO*; the
"static" of "Tomorrow, Tomorrow," and the everpre-
sent "night" literally *build* a space; a physical manifestation of Smith's "airless cell." The *Basement* version of
"Memory Lane" cleverly extends Smith's literalization
of its central metaphor and further emphasizes the

dangers of the past, but these early live versions make for an interesting addition to Smith's *XO*-era oeuvre.

Miss Misery [Released on
the *Good Will Hunting* Soundtrack]

In many ways, "Miss Misery" is inseparable from *XO*, though it was not included on the record itself. Larry Crane describes it as "the song that was almost on *XO* that wasn't":

> It kind of really ties together well with that record, it was just such an albatross at that point. You know, just eclipsing everything is this one stupid song that was just a demo, ostensibly. And now [for Elliott] you're doing an hour's worth of interviews about this thing while you're trying to make *XO*. While I was visiting Sunset Sound that week they made the move to drop "Miss Misery" from the running order of *XO*.

As with many songs from its era, "Miss Misery" underwent a series of notable changes, both musically and lyrically, before its completion. The earliest extant version of the song, released on the excellent *New Moon* compilation, contains an entirely different chorus: "But it's alright / 'cause some enchanted night I'll be with you." The sweetness of Smith's voice elevates these lines above simple cliché, but they fail to signify much beyond a utilitarian rock and roll chorus.

The song's first bridge, which arrives disarmingly soon in its overall arc, initially read "the tarot cards and the lines in my hand / Tell me I'm wrong but they're untrue." By the second studio version of "Miss Misery," this line—which initially seems like a very long way to say "I'm right"—has been given characters and a narrative. The transition from the song's first bridge to its second verse mobilizes an almost dream-like shift in subjectivity; the bridge involves talking to a "man in the park," who reads Smith's palm and tells him that he's "strong, hardly ever wrong," to which Smith replies "man, you mean you." That "you" then becomes the first line of the next verse, "you had plans for both of us that involved a trip out of town." A return to the song's opening chord evokes a sense of waking up; that mysterious "man in the park" is only a temporary break from the play of characters central to the song. The most narratively specific portions of Smith's songs are often the most surreal and hallucinatory.

The final lines of "Miss Misery" were subject to a similarly fruitful series of refinements. In the song's earliest incarnation, Smith prefaced its final chorus with "and I cried to see when you talked to me the night you said we were through," a line that veers toward cliché, both descriptively and sentimentally. As it appears on the *Good Will Hunting* soundtrack, these lines hit with the self-explanatory emotional specificity described by Darnielle:

> To vanish into oblivion is easy to do
> And I try to be, but you know me I come back
>   when you want me to
> Do you miss me, miss misery
> Like you say you do?

In its final repetition, the song's inquisitive chorus has been dramatically recast by the lyrics preceding it. Smith has revealed his dependence upon the song's subject, but also his awareness of that dependence; emotional intelligence set against an uncontrollable emotional addiction.

"Miss Misery" is a beautiful song, a rich and complicated interpersonal tale that is in fact, quite representative of Smith's work. But its relationship to his musical legacy is, as Crane suggests, complicated as well. Smith was fascinated with contradictions, and the success of "Miss Misery" makes for a great one; it is at once remarkable (a song as understated and affectively intricate as "Miss Misery" being nominated for an Oscar) and unremarkable (a contracted professional songwriter being recognized for a soundtrack contribution). It is also predicated upon a necessary white lie; though the song was written and tracked before Van Sant ever heard it, Smith had to pretend that it was written "for" the film to see it nominated. In the next section of this book, I examine how Smith came to be constructed in popular culture through the success of "Miss Misery," and how that construction was read over and against *XO*.

Part Two—"Pictures of Me"

In 1997, Elliott Smith was a respected but largely unknown professional musician who had released three albums (one on a major label) with his recently disbanded group Heatmiser, and three increasingly ornate and well-received solo albums. In 1998, Elliott Smith was an undiscovered, strung out coffee house troubadour plucked from obscurity by director Gus Van Sant.

How did this happen?

Or, to take a step back; why even bother discussing it? If Elliott Smith's music stands in such stark opposition to his popular image, why waste time even addressing the latter?

The answer is, simply, that I don't believe that the process of hearing a record is ever an unmediated one. One can come to an understanding of a record that does not match up with that record's cultural

positioning, but the two can never fully be disso-
ciated. As I have found in my own experience with
Smith's music, the way a musician's name circulates
(or that of an author or visual artist) can greatly affect
the way his/her music is heard.

Furthermore, an in-depth and systematic analysis
serves to move the discussion away from one about
which writers "get it" and which writers don't. My
interest in citing numerous articles surrounding the
release of *XO* is not to call out any particular writers
for buying into any one "story" of Elliott Smith, or for
failing to understand the "truth" of his work, but rather
to examine how these "stories" came to be and how
they developed over time. Indeed, I am hard pressed to
imagine how a 500-word newspaper article that does *not*
play into Smith's popular mythology could be deemed
editorially relevant. The "story" of Elliott Smith is one
that we as a culture have *all* told, enjoyed and contrib-
uted to, but the print media offers us a unique chance
to take apart and examine the rhetorical engines that
power Smith's popular construction.

In his popular music theory primer, Keith Negus
works toward establishing a critical framework for
how this dynamic can be understood:

Although mediation has often been used in an elusive
way and is sometimes a vaguely defined concept, it is

one that I am using to stress how popular music cannot be known in any neutral, immediate or naively experiential way. I am using the idea of mediation to stress that human experiences are grounded in cultural activities which are understood and given meaning through particular languages and symbols. . . . We may, somewhere deep inside, "feel" and "know" music in a quite profound way . . . However, as soon as we try to communicate and share this experience we are caught up in language and culture—the range of concepts, communicative actions and social practices that we must use to formulate convey and exchange meanings with other people.

In defining music as inseparable from mediation, Negus moves against the trend toward viewing mediation as that which *hinders* or *interferes with* our ability to objectively experience music. Indeed, Negus suggests that there is really no such thing as "objective" listening, at least in the way that it is popularly conceived; instead, the process of listening to music is always social and cultural.

This idea helps to erode problematic theoretical differentiation between "real" music fans and casual music listeners. Pop music theory is marked by a history of such binary oppositions; art vs. commerce, active vs. passive. Theodore Adorno, the great grandfather of academic music criticism, wrote extensively of music fans being fundamentally "duped" by the popular music apparatus. David Reisman amended Adorno's critical framework to include the "subcultural" listener, a music fan too hip and savvy to be fooled by the vast capitalist machinations of the culture industry. This mode of thought has its cultural legacy in the distinction between those listeners who are smart and interested enough to see past social, cultural, and industrial cues ("real fans"), and those who blindly follow them.

Negus's theoretical approach suggests not only that listening is an essentially active experience, but also that it is in fact inseparable from the forces that theoretically ensnare the "passive" listener. In *Music Genres and Corporate Cultures*, Negus expands his argument to address how specific genres of music can bring to bear their own processes of cultural mediation. He positions the term "genre" not as a strict aesthetic codification, but rather as a set of interpretive expectations:

> In using the term "genre culture" I am drawing on Steve Neale's use of genre as a sociological rather than formal concept, "not . . . as forms of textual codifications, but as systems of orientations, expectations and conventions that circulate between industry, text and subject" (Neale, 1980, p. 1p). One of the most obvious ways that these expectations may circulate is through the institutionalized system of media, particularly

radio and video, and the way this contributes to the definition and boundaries of what falls within and without a genre of music.

Negus's formulation of genre (itself based on the work of a film scholar, not a music scholar) goes beyond the use of the term to denote a naturally unified aesthetic or "sound." To see this theory put to practice, one need not look farther than Elliott Smith's oft-assigned genre: "singer/songwriter." Technically speaking, the term is an occupational/biographical description more so than an aesthetic one. And while this generic distinction may have its origins in the aesthetic of Smith's early work, it also served to cast him as a figure of pure, "authentic" confessional expression, set against the decidedly inauthentic world of the Academy Awards.

Negus cites Richard A. Peterson's construction of "authenticity" as crucial in how genre issues are communicated. In his study *Creating Country Music: Fabricating Authenticity,* Peterson describes in detail the processes by which "authentic" country music has been defined and reshaped over time.

The ironic phrase "fabricating authenticity" is used here to highlight the fact that authenticity is not inherent in the object or event that is designated authentic but is a socially agreed-upon construct in which the past is to a degree misremembered (Hawlbachs 1992) . . . Unlike these other situations that have been researched, no authority is in a position to dictate authenticity in country music. Rather, as we will discover in the chapters that follow, it is continuously negotiated in an ongoing interplay between performers, diverse commercial interests, fans, and the evolving image.

Peterson's use of the phrase "socially agreed-upon" is intentionally and productively vague; indeed, there is no single party that can bestow "authenticity." Nor, as I have suggested, is "authenticity" simply a fallacy embraced by those dastardly writers who don't "understand" Smith's work exactly the way I do. "Authenticity" is, in many ways, a necessary cultural construct, one that often seems to work *against* hegemony precisely because it cannot be conferred by any one authority. Toilet paper jingles hatched in a corporate boardroom and pop songs crafted in a barren bedroom are both written to tug at our heartstrings. The imperfect and illusory construct of a bottom-up consensus is one way to filter the incessant stream of stimuli we are confronted with—a flawed but well-intentioned way to decide what we will "trust" to move, repulse or inspire us.

Of course "authenticity," like any other cultural construct, is highly manipulable. Negus and Peterson both primarily address ways in which a musician's perceived "authenticity" can be shaped and directed by those who stand to make a profit. But in the case of Elliott Smith, there seems to have been no such attempt by DreamWorks, Smith's management, or Smith himself to present himself as an "authentic" singer/songwriter—or an "authentic" anything, for that matter. In nearly every interview from the time of *XO*, Smith flatly rejected the "singer/songwriter" tag.

If Smith and those who stood to profit from him did *not* present him as an "authentic" singer/songwriter, how did this construct come to inform his popular image? And how did this construct inform the perceived continuities and disjuncts between Smith's biography and his musical output?

Just as Negus did in his definition of "genre," I turn here to the work of a film scholar. John Ellis, who has written extensively on the issue of stardom, describes how an actor's "star image" can provide a kind of *fore*knowledge to that actor's films:

> Stars have a similar function in the film industry to the creation of a "narrative image": they provide a foreknowledge of the fiction, an invitation to cinema. Stars are incomplete images outside the cinema: the performance of the film is the moment of completion of images in subsidiary circulation, in newspaper, fanzines, etc. Further, a paradox is present in

these subsidiary forms. The star is at once ordinary and extraordinary, available for desire and unattainable . . . Furthermore, the star's particular performance in a film is always more than the culmination of the star images in subsidiary circulation: it is a balancing act between fiction and cultism.

Ellis continues: "It may well be that a similar creation of stars is impossible for broadcast TV (which fosters 'personalities'), but does take place in the rock music industry." Indeed, star studies provides a fruitful and productive lens for examining how a figure like Smith is created in the popular consciousness, and how his music can come to be the crux by which that popular image *must* be realized and validated.

The overarching difference between film and music, of course, is that film is understood to be mimetic and fictional; certainly, nobody thinks that a famous actor and one of his roles are *actually* the same. What stardom studies suggests, however, is that the star's cultural image—articulated in "newspapers, fanzines, etc"—provides a context for understanding the fictional film; a context that is utilized in promoting the film, and in many ways necessary for understanding the film. This dynamic seems more unencumbered in popular music, as there is often no presumed difference between the star and his or her role in the text.

With these critical lenses applied, one begins to see how both Smith's "life story" ("star image") *and* popular readings of his music ("narrative image") could be simultaneously constructed through a sort of epistemological feedback loop. For Smith to be an "authentic" singer-songwriter, he must have *really experienced* the things he sings about—especially those that most mark him as "other" to the glitzy world of Hollywood. For the gratifying completion of Smith's "star image" to take place, his music must, in turn, reflect the biography offered in newspapers and magazines. For Smith to retain his "authenticity," that reading of his music must be verified by the "life story" told in newspapers and magazines. And so it goes.

On February 20, 1998, *Yahoo! Launch* ran a piece about Smith's Oscar nomination—one of the first to appear anywhere in the mainstream media. Discussing Smith's contributions to Gus Van Sant's popular Hollywood film, the article's writer retroactively constructs a "star image" for Smith via the "narrative image" of Matt Damon's Will Hunting:

> Maybe [Smith and Will Hunting] aren't so far apart; maybe Elliott Smith was so perfect for *Good Will Hunting* because, just like Will in the movie, while seen by society as a fuck-up, he's a genius working in obscurity who's suddenly given the chance to enter the mainstream. That is, if he can . . . and if he wants to.

A number of assumptions are passively enacted here; most notably, that Smith is "seen by society as a fuck-up." *Who* exactly sees Smith as a fuck-up is not specified—the narrative of Smith's meteoric and unprecedented ascent is, in a sense, already written: just as Sean Maguire acknowledged and elevated Will Hunting's scorned and untapped genius, we can *all* acknowledge and elevate Elliott Smith's.

The problem, of course, is that Smith's genius was not all that untapped, nor his ascent all that meteoric or unprecedented. By and large, "society" didn't see Elliott Smith at all, and among those who did, he was well respected for his musical talent. Having already released on album on one major label and signed a contract with another, any claim to Smith's absolute "obscurity" is more than a little bit dubious. But the story of the unrecognized, "authentic" genius suddenly thrust into the national spotlight is an irresistible one.

On March 20, 1998, this "authentic genius" was introduced to the country at large; Smith was written up in an extensive *USA Today* article that reads as a kind of primer on the deferrals and paradoxes inherent to Smith's cultural positioning. As with the *Yahoo! Launch* piece, it introduces Smith as a singer "plucked out of obscurity and plunked smack into Oscar hubbub." The article goes on to say that Smith "has been described as an acerbic poet and street bohemian who writes sad folk songs." Smith's self-description as "pop . . . I like melodies" does little to drown out the unspecified throngs who apparently perceive him as an "acerbic poet." Once again, an uncredited passive voice is used to describe Smith to an audience that is likely quite unfamiliar with his work. Needless to say, I have not been able to find a single article that explicitly names Smith as a "street bohemian."

An April 1998 article in the *LA Times* expounded a bit upon what exactly the life of a newly elevated "street bohemian" might look like:

> A few weeks ago, Elliott Smith performed his Oscar-nominated song "Miss Misery" for more than 55 million on the Academy Awards telecast. A month earlier, he was playing the tiny L.A. Rock club Spaceland. A year ago he was trying to kill himself.

Here again, Smith's "authenticity" is posed as a direct counterpoint to the inauthentic Academy Awards. And, as would often be the case, allusions to suicide attempts—or heroin use—are offered as irrefutable proof of such authenticity. (Both of these subjects have long been used as rhetorical shortcuts to "authenticity" for many artists, writers, and musicians.) Doubtless, the fact that Smith broached these subjects in his lyrics made it all the more necessary for suicide and drug abuse to be constructed as an integral part of his life story, as his status as an "authentic" singer-songwriter was predicated upon his musical expression being "real" and "genuine." Besides, if the aestheticization and idolization of a singer's image—like that of Celine Dion—render an artist shallow and false, then what could be more "authentic" than utter self-annihilation?

In her article "Art Versus Commerce: Deconstructing a (Useful) Romantic Illusion," Deena Weinstein suggests that drug use and suicide are common discursive tools for constructing the romantic myth of the artist:

> Critics celebrate romantic rock deaths because they affirm the myth of the artist. A drug overdose, a shotgun suicide, or a gangland gangsta slaying; these deaths show, rhetorically, that the romantic artist was authentic, not merely assuming a (Christlike) pose. The right kind of death is the most powerful authenticity effect, the indefeasible outward sign of inward grace. "The artist must be sacrificed to their art; like the bees they must but their lives into the sting they give," Ralph Waldo Emerson wrote. . . . Death isn't the only authenticity effect embraced by rock writers. They also champion heroin-addicted musicians and rockers who are off their rockers. . . . Addicts and insane are automatically authentic because their grip on rationality is too weak to allow them to "sell out."

Thus, in the wake of his Oscar performance, Smith's "star image," as articulated in the news media, was that of the sad, suicidal sap, suddenly (and perhaps unwantedly) thrust into the national spotlight. His extensive back catalog, its enthusiastic reception, and its modest commercial success often get entirely omitted. Reputable labels (Kill Rock Stars) and sizeable clubs (Spaceland) are suddenly "tiny." And—most troubling of all—Smith himself is positioned as a suicidal "fuck-up," whose "sudden" success as a musician is in no way the result of hard work, perseverance or—God forbid—ambition (I mean, the guy tried to *kill* himself!).

As Ellis suggested, however, such "star images" are incomplete without that star's texts. In both the *Yahoo! Launch* and *LA Times* pieces, *Good Will Hunting* itself is positioned as such a text. The May 30, 1998 UK release of *Either/Or* offered a preliminary glimpse of how Smith's music would be read against his new-found popular construction. A column in the UK's *Times* includes a near-hallucinatory reading of Smith's music, and its positioning against the "hysterical" artifice of Celine Dion:

> You just don't meet Oscar-nominated songwriters who aren't Celine Dion. And, unlike Dion, her 17 producers and her hysterical 1,600-piece orchestra, "Miss Misery," like all Smith songs, is just Smith and his guitar. Finger-picked Nick Drake melancholia.

> Vague country-folk, washed in inky blue blues, like Simon and Garfunkel trying to be Big Stars.

The equation of Smith's music with "Nick Drake melancholia"—ostensibly in a review of an album thick with electric guitar, bass, drum, and keyboards— seems rooted in more in Smith's popular construction as a Nick Drake-esque folk antihero than in the music itself. A review in the London *Independent* tows a similar line, opening with a picture of Celine Dion and Smith standing side-by-side at the Academy Awards: "the glittery, coiffured diva and the nervous, slowly spoken singer who etched out his career playing in the quirky and eclectic underground scene of Portland, Oregon." Once again, Nick Drake is invoked as a point of reference:

> For someone who delivers haunting tales of truncated, druggy relationships set to a mostly acoustic sound- scape and delivered in fragile whispering tones, Smith's rave notices in the US press have often harked on about Nick Drake or other folk or singer-songwriting legends. It's not something he seems to cherish.

This curiously anthropological-sounding observation ushers in an extensive quote from Smith, explaining that he is "neither folk nor singer-songwriter," and that he's always had a preference for "punk bands."

The piece resumes, "In any case, Smith's music is undeniably late-Nineties in tone." Though I'm still not entirely sure what "late-nineties in tone" means, the description itself seems less telling than the odd dismissal that precedes it. The presence of a quotation from Smith himself gives the article an air of authority and veracity, which is in turn used to sacrifice Smith's voice to his cultural myth.

These rhetorical strategies carried over into the flurry of press surrounding *XO*'s release. An August 1 article in *Billboard* magazine already differs sharply in tone from an earlier Billboard piece from February 21 of that same year. While the earlier piece immediately mentions Heatmiser, and discusses the relative success of *Either/Or*, the August 1 piece responds to a perceived need to establish continuity between *XO* and Smith's earlier work:

> *XO* comprises more full-band material—featuring Smith playing most instruments—while retaining the intimacy and immediacy of his solo acoustic work. *XO* is still clearly an Elliott Smith record, with its share of quiet acoustic numbers, detours into time, and songs about love, longing, and drunken stupor.

Here, the essence of an "Elliott Smith record" is reduced to its "quiet acoustic numbers," even though the record preceding *XO* was by no means a "quiet acoustic" record. (Nor, for that matter, was "Miss Misery" a "quiet acoustic" song.) An August 25 piece in the *Toronto Star* describes Smith's music as "stark, mostly-acoustic, confessional-feeling tales of drug addiction, failed romance, and existential turmoil." An August 29 article in the *Globe and Mail* mentions Smith's "intimate, poetic folk muse." For Smith's music to effectively complete his "star image" (and for it to remain newsworthy), it must be continually constructed as *other* to the perceived excess of pop music.

As Smith's music grew even farther away from the aesthetic mold of the "folk singer" or "singer/songwriter," an odd current of personal antagonism began to emerge in the press. A review of *XO* in the *New York Daily News* exemplifies the increasingly harsh and belittling language used to describe Smith. Setting the scene, as such reviews almost invariably did, with a picture of Smith's Oscar performance, the article describes how "a greasy weed of a man murmured his eerie ballad 'Miss Misery,' about a depressed alcoholic, on the same stage occupied minutes earlier by such commercial titans as Celine Dion and LeAnn Rimes." The article goes on to say, "such delicious incongruity never would have happened if it weren't for director Gus Van Sant, who plucked Smith from the hip hinterlands to grace his soundtrack to 'Good Will Hunting.'" *XO*, with its impeccable production values and forceful rock and roll arrangements, threatened to undermine this very "delicious incongruity," perhaps accounting for the newfound emphasis on Smith's personal life it seems to have triggered in the mainstream press.

A *Boston Globe* show review describes the "scraggly-haired" Smith, who "no one's every going to confuse . . . with the happiest boy in the room," and suggests that even as *XO* is a more optimistic record, "if you grasp what Smith's singing, you hear the gritty imagery under the chiming chords and even-keeled tempos." The vague shorthand "gritty" signifies barely anything if not fleshed out by some understanding of Smith's popular image. And, once again, the suggestion that this "gritty imagery" is the part of Smith's music that needs to be "grasped" swiftly dismisses the album's remarkable musical achievement as something that needs to be overcome to get to the "real" nature of Smith's songwriting.

By late 1998, the press seems to have grown frustrated and impatient with Smith's unwillingness to accept the "singer/songwriter" tag—a frustration no doubt enhanced by the punked-up renditions of *XO* tunes that Smith was performing with Sam Coomes and Janet Weiss of Quasi as his backing band. In an *Irish Times* article previewing a December 6 show, Smith is quoted extensively as wanting to escape the "singer/songwriter" tag. The article retorts, ". . . that seems unlikely. Smith is shy and self-effacing—and the songs cover the usual songwriter territory of alienation and self-doubt. The difference is that not every songwriter can so successfully transform such frustration into something of beauty." It is often directly before or after a quote in which Smith rejects the "singer/songwriter" role that he is described as "shy," "self-effacing," "soft-spoken." Even if he doesn't see himself as a "singer/songwriter," it is clear that *we all* do, and it is clear why we should.

A follow-up on *Yahoo! Launch* from October of 1998 repeats the deferrals of the earlier piece:

> You can't read about Elliott Smith without running across phrases like "reclusive, tortured artiste" and "sad, haunting songs." As a result, there's a prevailing public image of Smith as some kind of brooding and brokenhearted waif-man perfect in his misery, a writer of beautiful melancholy music but not exactly the type of guy you want manning the phones at Suicide Prevention.

Once again, Smith expresses his frustration at being painted as a "morose folk singer." Once again, the writer responds incredulously:

> Well, you're probably thinking, you do play acoustic guitar and write lyrics like "Here's the

silhouette/ The face always turned away/ The bleeding color gone to black/ Dying like the day" (from "Oh Well, Okay"), sooo . . .

Indeed, as Smith's music grew farther away from the "singer/songwriter" mold, his lyrics became a more common means of asserting that he *is*, in fact, a real-life "tortured singer-songwriter," despite his protestations. An extensive feature in the January 1999 issue of *Spin* equates one of Smith's song titles with his supposed suicide attempt:

> Massaging a glass of beer, he seems happy, truly happy, which is not something a singer/songwriter so often linked with words such as "gloom" and "Garfunkel" is supposed to be. Happier than someone who sings about the need to "Bottle Up and Explode," and happier than someone who last year tried to kill himself.

Indeed, by early-to-mid-1999, many articles written about Smith made a point of ostensibly refuting the idea that Smith is "sad" or "depressed," even as they suggested that it is unavoidable to draw such a conclusion from Smith's music. A piece from the *Washington Post* insists that Smith is "not sad," but goes on to describe him in very similar terms to those that are then deferred onto the ambiguous "listeners":

> Elliott Smith is not sad. He sounds a bit withdrawn as he haltingly answers questions by phone from a West Coast hotel room, and he's so soft-spoken that his words barely register on tape. Still, he gently objects, he's not as "melancholy," "bleak," or "dark"—to use some of the more popular adjectives—as listeners often assume from his music.

A *Boston Globe* article parallels this progression:

> Elliott Smith is not a junkie. He's not desperately messed-up, at least not any more than anyone else. He claims to have written a happy song, and believes that his music seems a bit darker than most because for one thing, he doesn't have a band, and for another, he wouldn't dream of singing contrived lyrics that don't mean anything to him.

> Still, it's not hard to see why Smith has been cast in the role of tunesmith to the downtrodden alt-crowd. His records are filled with unflinching, emotionally raw portraits of drug addicts and alcoholics, and spare, poetic sketches of self-loathing and decayed love. . . . Listening to the songs is as lonely and solitary an endeavor as the lives his characters lead.

While we were once simply asked to assume that Smith was "seen as a fuck-up" or "described as an acerbic poet," the genesis of these beliefs is now traced back to—who else—Smith himself. Smith's music having been constructed as a corollary to his unattributed cultural reputation, it is now cited as the basis for that reputation. A May 2000 review of *Figure 8* in the *Boston Globe* summarizes and enacts this very process:

> The problem with being tunesmith to the downtrodden is that, for better or worse, you become your songs. It makes no difference that you consider yourself a storyteller, a chronicler of dreams, a poet who cobbles fragments of your life and other people's lives and an entirely made-up version of life. Your miserable fans (and even your well-adjusted fans who desperately crave a miserably authentic experience) need to believe that you are the junkie, you are the loser in love, you are the bruised, self-loathing misfit. And if you happen to be the sort of songwriter who can translate pain with the gentle intelligence of Simon and Garfunkel, the epic pop songcraft of the Beatles, and the skewed, raw edge of the indie-rock scene that spawned you—there's no escaping the microscope.

Finally, the process comes full-circle. Smith's positioning as an authentically "fucked up" "singer/songwriter," set against the inauthentic artifice of the Academy Awards, formed the basis for a common reading of his music. That reading, in turn, informed a series of assumptions and projections regarding Smith's motivations, demeanor, biography, and fan base. These maneuvers electrified a powerful, closed circuit of meaning between creator ("reclusive, tortured artiste") and creative product ("portraits of drug addicts and alcoholics").

If, as I have suggested, *XO* explicitly shorts that circuit, and does so via an aesthetic that does *not* align easily with the "folk" "singer/songwriter," why was it so often positioned in service of this popular myth?

One answer can be found in idea, expressed in the *Globe* piece and many others, that Smith's gift was one for "[translating] pain." In their ambitious and rewarding examination of *Creativity, Communication and Cultural Value*, Negus and Michael Pickering deconstruct the commonly held idea that creativity is a simple codification of preexisting experiences and emotions:

> People do not—as artists, writers, musicians—have some pre-formed condition that they then seek to express in an art form and communicate to others. The contours and characteristics of experience are given meaning and value through the process of expression and communication . . .
>
> A songwriter may decide to write a sad song, regardless of how they're feeling at that moment. A painter may wish to convey a sense of anger at the atrocities of war. We may hear the song or see the painting and interpret it as an example of someone condensing their experience into song form or pictoral representation

and then relaying it to us. But the act of expressing whatever sadness or anger we may recognize and relate to is realized in the act of making the song and painting. It doesn't exist in some pure or prior state which words, music or paint then approximate in some way or other.

This myth of creativity intersects with Negus's inclusive and insightful definition of genre as a series of culturally agreed upon expectations; indeed, different "genres" rely upon and activate this particular construction of creativity in different ways. Broadly speaking, those musicians whose "genre" casts them as musical innovators or cultural pastiche artists are not necessarily presumed to be expressing some deeply held emotion or experience. By contrast, the "folk," "acoustic" or "singer/songwriter" genre construct is often presumed to be the most directly confessional. When postmodern posterboy Beck released the more conventionally "folky" *Sea Change* in 2002, it was suddenly held as a shining example of personal "truth" put to music, dramatically recasting the type of "creativity" credited to artist who had previously been seen primarily as a clever aesthetic manipulator. *Rolling Stone* called *Sea Change* "an impeccable album of truth and light [created] from the end of love." Nobody seemed particularly interested in what emotional experience(s) may have informed *Midnite Vultures*, nor in the possibility that *Sea Change* was simply another genre experiment from one of pop music's most dexterous stylistic chameleons.

Indeed, while Beck has his roots in the self-proclaimed "anti-folk" scene and helped to usher in the playful aesthetic irreverence of the mid-to-late 1990s, even he could not escape some of the longest standing cultural assumptions about creative production. The mythology surrounding the "author" is central to modern cultural studies, and forms the basis for many of the ideas set forth by scholars such as Ellis and Negus. In the seminal essay "The Death of the Author," Roland Barthes discusses at length the way that literary criticism privileges knowledge about the author him/herself as a means of interpreting a work:

> The *author* still reigns in histories of literature, biographies of writers, interviews, magazines, and in the very consciousness of men of letters anxious to unite their person and their work through diaries and memoirs. The image of literature to be found in ordinary culture is tyrannically centered on the author, his person, his life, his tastes, his passion, while criticism still consists for the most part in saying that Baudelaire's work is the failure of Baudelaire the man, Van Gogh's his madness, Tchaikovsky's his vice. The *explanation* of a work is always sought in the man or woman who produced it, as if it were always

in the end, through the more or less transparent alle-
gory of the fiction, the voice of a single person, the
author "confiding" in us.

Barthes goes on to explain how this sort of interpretation is advantageous to the critic, giving him/her
a clear set of criteria by which to validate his or her
opinion.

Once the author is removed, the claim to decipher a
text becomes quite futile. To give a text an Author
is to impose a limit on that text, to furnish it with a
final signified, to close the writing. Such a conception suits criticism very well, the latter then allotting
itself the important task of discovering the Author
(or its hypostases: society, history, psyche, liberty)
beneath the work: when the Author has been found,
the text is "explained"—victory to the critic.

To expand Barthes' assertion with the modern aph-
orism "everybody's a critic" is to understand part of
what we stand to lose by disjoining Smith's craft and
his biography. The process of uncovering the "truth"
behind a piece of art is gratifying for *everybody* and, in
the information age, a pursuit that is by no means limited to critics or "men of letters." Ironically, the bur-
geoning online media democracy seems only to have
exaggerated this effect; as blogs and message boards
offer up innumerable, conflicting interpretations of

creative work, the urge to fix a piece of art to its "true" meaning is more prevalent than ever.

If we are to give up the quest to fix Smith's music in its "true" meaning, we must also give up the romantic illusion that this meaning is only accessible to a select few "true" fans, or to those who knew Smith personally. To do so is both to draw a tenuous interpretive perimeter around Smith's work itself, and to accept that the potential meanings that exist within that perimeter are limitless. In doing so, we recast Smith not as a rarified genius whose artistic concerns are beyond our understanding, but rather as a skilled, dedicated, and fallible craftsman whose work we can all discuss, interpret and enjoy. The myth of Smith's "genius" explodes his agency; he is at once omnipotent and impotent, blessed with a preternatural gift that was somehow beyond his control or understanding. (In one of the more darkly romantic iterations of this myth, this blessing inevitably becomes the curse that leads to the artist's tragic downfall.) Crane suggests that it was hard work, not some unquantifiable spark of "genius," that ultimately elevated Smith's musical output to the stellar heights of *XO*:

> I was just reading *This Is Your Brain on Music* by Daniel J. Levitin.... There are no geniuses, but there people that are called "geniuses." In every case, it's

10,000 hours of practice before anybody ever starts to say that. And that's got to be the case with [Elliott]. I remember we were tracking one song, playing it on guitar, and he goes, "eh, I'm not sure if this is working out. Maybe I'll try it on piano." And he just walks over to the piano, and plays the song perfectly, top to bottom. And I know he hadn't practiced it; he was just able to transcribe it in his head, and then really play it on the piano—we're talking left and right hand and everything. And then he could walk over and play it on drums. And it's because he's already done that work—he'd recorded thousands of hours of stuff that no one needs to hear.

Indeed, among the countless live and demo recordings I have pored over, there are some true clunkers—awkward, inelegant, obvious, and cloying musical and lyrical snippets born of the same creative mind that gave us *XO*. Smith, like all of us, was given to his share of good ideas and his share of bad ideas. It is impressive, to say the least, that Smith conjured enough critical distance from his own work to distill a glut of demo recordings and unfinished songs into a handful of concise and unerringly strong records.

It is also impressive that an artist as clever and self-aware as Smith never released an album that intentionally and explicitly sought to counter his popular construction—no *Get Happy!*-esque retort to the critics who saw him as a one-dimensional caricature.

In an interview with *Salon.com*, Smith demonstrated a keen awareness of his own popular image, and of how that image differed from his own understanding of his music:

> I just make up songs that to me feel human. And they're bound to be seen by some people as confessional or depressing, some sort of real one-way assessment that is not how they are to me. . . . And it's really easy not to worry about all that, except for the persistent questions that come up. Maybe not in this interview, but in a lot of them. "Why are you so sad?" . . . There must be some reason why I always get these questions, which to me seem like totally surface things about my music. There's a lot in my music that I find happy and optimistic, in both the melody and the lyrics.

Just as every single one of Smith's records is cited in support of his cultural myth, every single one of Smith's records is subtle and substantive enough to outlast it. Smith was not afraid to take his cues from timeless, canonical albums—the very kind that are often seen as critically and creatively unapproachable on account of their creators' singular "genius." Smith detested artistic self-importance, but he was never afraid to take his *work* seriously—to listen, write, think, and edit until he crafted a record that could hold its own among those he most admired. It is an approach too inclusive, too pragmatic, and too daunting to be the stuff of cultural myth. Instead—like *XO* itself—it is improbably, beautifully, real.

* * *

Ghosts may not exist as metaphysical apparitions, but they do exist as semantic artifacts. Any piece of writing about an artist like Smith is, in a sense, haunted. Smith's death hangs heavy over every line of his lyrics, and every word written about him. Aside from the insurmountable sadness of a creative life cut short, Smith's untimely death seemed only to validate the mythology surrounding his body of work. As an end point to the narrative of the "tortured singer-songwriter," it could not be more fitting; some pieces written after Smith's death read as "I told you so" as much as they did "I'm sorry." Many brief obituaries offered only a sad, shallow glimpse into a wonderfully rich creative life: "singer-songwriter who struggled with drug addiction." Or, in the words of the UK *Guardian*, "No one was too surprised when Elliott Smith—a boozy, druggy Oscar-nominated folk singer who had talked openly about killing himself—was found dead."

These articles are problematic not because they overstate the extent of Smith's personal troubles (which, again, I don't see fit to comment upon here), but rather because they insist upon a particular correlation between the darker parts of Smith's biography and the whole of his musical output. This correlation inevitably sparked a search for "clues" in Smith's lyrics; when *New Moon* was released in 2006, internet forums were abuzz with discussion of the already-long-leaked "Georgia, Georgia," and its lyric "Oh man, what a plan, suicide." Most of this chatter omitted the line's conclusion, ". . . it's just not that much different from my own affair," which positions its subject matter as metaphorical, not confessional. Indeed, Smith's interest in themes of drug addiction and suicide was not simply a reflection of his personal opinions on these subjects, let alone his personal experiences. These issues in and of themselves never seemed to be of much interest to Smith; it was their bearing on bigger questions of agency, intellect, and emotion that intrigued him. (Smith was, after all, a student of philosophy and the son of a psychiatrist.)

As I have suggested, this tension between rational thought, creativity, and experience is not simply a passing thematic concern of Smith's; it is at the very core of his lyrical approach and musical philosophy. Smith's reliance upon a simple and straightforward vocabulary often masks the complex and consistent internal language of his work, not to mention his unerring precision as a lyricist. Few musicians manage to write with Smith's pinpoint emotional accuracy, and fewer still manage to do so without sacrificing the coherency of their work as pop music.

Ultimately, the distinction that must be made is that between the craftsman and the craft itself. The particulars of how the "real life" of Elliott Smith informed his work are not really accessible to anybody other than Smith himself, who insisted both in interviews and in his music that personal struggle does not translate into great art. Indeed, as Negus suggests, the very idea that art is a mere transposition of preexisting emotions and experience is a fallacy. The urge to understand Smith as a human being is by no means an innately ghoulish one; Autumn de Wilde's picture and interview book does a great job of providing nonlinear glimpses into Elliott Smith's life via people who knew him. It is the urge to reduce his life into a cartoonish narrative, then read that narrative back into his music, that threatens to bleed the color, life, and complexity from an amazing body of work.

De Wilde's book is interesting largely because it consists largely of interviews with artists and musicians. The "Elliott Smith" who exists as a ghastly foregone conclusion seems very different from the Elliott Smith treasured by fans and musicians alike. Indeed, many of the most interesting conversations I've had about

Smith's music have been with musicians; Smith's work ethic, craft, and formal discipline are tremendously inspiring. Still, I doubt that Smith will ever be categorized as a hugely influential musician; his work is at once too musically unique and too aesthetically broad to fit into any clear lineage. Elliott Smith will never really be owned by the history of "acoustic" music or "folk" music or "lo-fi" music, or even "pop" music—his work will always be, simply, Elliott Smith music.

Indeed, while Smith is often invoked as a cautionary figure, his devotion to songcraft was nothing short of instructive. In an interview with *Comes With a Smile*, friend and frequent musical collaborator Sam Coomes described watching Smith come into his own as a musician:

> I've known Elliott for a long time. And when I first met him I thought he was a talented musician—but I know a lot of talented musicians; I never thought he was the *most* talented or anything. But he's just pushed himself and grown as a musician pretty intensely over the years and I've been able to watch it from close range and that's extremely instructive—musically— but it's also gratifying to see a friend and associate pick himself up like that and get a wider recognition.

Smith worked tirelessly to make himself a better musician, and the result of that work lives on, strong and stunning as ever. *XO* stands as a tremendously powerful statement that art can transcend and outlive the difficulties we face; that even if a writer is "stuck inside [his] imagination," the products of that stasis can be remarkable. Focusing on the supposed tragedy of Smith's personal life serves only to rarify his suffering and belittle his creative achievements. There is no dearth of pain and sadness in the world, but there are very few albums as singular and exquisite as *XO*.

Sources

Larry Crane was extremely helpful in constructing a timeline for the events leading up to *XO*'s release; I hope I have accurately reflected the information he provided.

Philip Fischer meticulously compiled and transcribed the live and demo recordings addressed in this book.

Whenever possible, lyrics cited are verified by official materials. Unverified lyrics were transcribed by myself and/or Philip Fischer.

[Author Unknown] "Elliott Smith," *Guitar Player*, September 1998.

[Author Unknown] "Luke Wood," *Record Labels and Companies Guide* [http://www.record-labels-companies-guide.com/interview-dreamworks.html].

Anderman, Joan, "Tunesmith to the Miserable," *The Boston Globe*, March 26, 1999.

Anderman, Joan, "Elliott Smith: Unfazed Songwriter Embraces His Beloved Outsider Mantle with 'Figure 8'," *The Boston Globe*, May 12, 2000.

Barrie, J. M., *Peter Pan.*

Barthes, Roland, "The Death of the Author," in *Image, Music, Text* (Noonday Press, 1977).

Bates, Jim, "Walkin' After Midnight," *Jim*, November 6, 1997.

Chelin, Pamela, "Elliott Smith," *The Big Takeover* no. 43, late 1998.

Cromelin, Richard, "'Misery' Has Company," *The LA Times*, April 19, 1998.

Darnielle, John, "Roman Candle," *Last Plane to Jakarta*, Spring 1998.

de Wilde, Autumn, *Elliott Smith* (Chronicle Books, 2007).

Dornan, Matt, "Elliott Smith," *Comes with a Smile*, Winter 1998/1999.

Ellis, John, "Stars as Cinematic Phenomenon," in Butler, Jeremy, *Star Texts: Image & Performance in Film & Television* (Wayne State University Press, 1991).

Farber, Jim, "Folkie Swings Into Pop," *New York Daily News*, September 6, 1998.

Filene, Benjamin, *Romancing the Folk: Public Memory & American Roots Music* (UNC Press, 2000).

Fricke, David, "*Sea Change*," *Rolling Stone*, October 3, 2002.

Fritch, Matthew, "Down on the Upside," *Magnet*, September/October 1998.

Greenfield-Sanders, Timothy, "The Delicate Sound of an Explosion," *Interview*, August 1998.

Hundley, Jessica, "Mr. Misery, He's Not," *Salon.com*, May 1, 2000.

Jenkins, Mark, "Elliott Smith's Emotional Snapshots," *The Washington Post*, March 19, 1999.

Kellogg, Carolyn, "And the Winner Is . . .," *Launch: Music on Yahoo!*, February 24, 1998.

Kelly, John, "Dreaming Up a Song," *The Irish Times*, November 28, 1998.

Moon, Tom, "A Singer Gone Slick? Fans Needn't Worry," *The Philadelphia Inquirer*, October 5, 1998.

Moran, Caitlin, "The Yolk in the Egg-White of Life," *The Times*, May 29, 1998.

Moses, Michael, "Smithery Loves Company," *Launch: Music on Yahoo!*, November 19, 1998.

Negus, Keith, *Music Genres and Corporate Cultures* (Routledge, 1999).

Negus, Keith, *Popular Music in Theory* (Wesleyan University Press, 1996).

Negus, Keith and Pickering, Michael, *Creativity, Communication and Cultural Value* (Sage, 1994).

Nugent, Benjamin, *Elliott Smith and the Big Nothing* (Da Capo Press, 2005).

Peisner, David, "Elliott Smith: The Well Rounded Interview," *Well Rounded Entertainment*, 1998.

Perry, Tim, "An Academy Award Performance," *The Independent*, May 30, 1998.

Peterson, Richard A., *Creating Country Music: Fabricating Authenticity* (University of Chicago Press, 1997).

Powers, Ann, "Vulnerable No More: Gloomy Becomes a Tad Bouncy," *The New York Times*, May 23, 2000.

Punter, Jennie, "An Original Steps Awkwardly into the Light," *The Globe and Mail*, August 29, 1998.

Rayner, Ben, "Singer Thrust Into the Spotlight," *The Toronto Star*, August 25, 1998.

Rosen, Craig, "Capitol S'Track Boosts Elliott Smith," *Billboard*, February 21, 1998.

Siegler, Dylan, "Smith Follows Up 'Good Will' Boost— Oscar-Nominated Artist Makes DreamWorks Debut with *XO*," *Billboard*, August 1, 1998.

Smith, R. J., "Elliott Smith: He's Mr. Dyingly Sad, and You're Mystifyingly Glad," *Spin*, January 1999.

Sullivan, Jim, "Elliott Smith Takes the Low-Fi Road to Oscar," *The Boston Globe*, March 12, 1998.

Sullivan, Jim, "Smith lets 'Miss Misery' Sit Out His Paradise Set," *The Boston Globe*, October 7, 1998.

Thomas, Karen, "'Misery' Puts Songwriter in the Academy's Company" *USA Today*, March 20, 1998.

Weinstein, Deena, "Art Versus Commerce: Deconstructing a (Useful) Romantic Illusion," in Kelly, Karen and McDonnell, Evelyn, *Stars Don't Stand Still in the Sky: Music and Myth* (New York University Press, 1999).

Also available in this series: